Eyewitness
VOLCANO &
EARTHQUAKE

Vesuv. Ash rain of the eruption
(March 1944: days 22. 23 24. 25. 26)

Skull from Herculaneum

Lava bomb

Sulfur

Gray-Milne seismograph, 1885

Carbonized bread from Pompeii

Cut peridot

Gem-quality olivine

Cut and uncut diamond

Carbonized walnuts from Pompeii

Preserved eggs from Pompeii

Body cast from Pompeii

Pele's hair,
thin strands
of volcanic
glass

Eyewitness
VOLCANO &
EARTHQUAKE

Voyager 1
space probe

Written by
SUSANNA VAN ROSE

Bottle melted in
eruption of
Mount Pelée

Perfume bottle
melted in eruption
of Mount Pelée

Zhang Heng's
earthquake detector

DK Publishing, Inc.

Seneca, Roman philosopher who wrote about earthquake of CE 62

Title page from *Campi Phlegraei*

Fork and pocket watch damaged in eruption of Mount Pelée

DK

LONDON, NEW YORK, MELBOURNE, MUNICH, and DELHI

Project editor Scott Steedman
Art editor Christian Sévigny
Designer Yaël Freudmann
Managing editor Helen Parker
Managing art editor Julia Harris
Production Louise Barratt
Picture research Kathy Lockley
Special photography James Stevenson
Editorial consultants Professor John Guest and Dr. Robin Adams

REVISED EDITION
Managing editor Andrew Macintyre
Managing art editor Jane Thomas
Editor and reference compiler Francesca Baines
Art editor Catherine Goldsmith
Production Jenny Jacoby
Picture research Sarah Pownall
DTP designer Siu Yin Ho

U.S. editor Elizabeth Hester
Senior editor Beth Sutinis
Art director Dirk Kaufman
U.S. DTP designer Milos Orlovic
U.S. production Chris Avgherinos

Mining transit

This Eyewitness ® Guide has been conceived by
Dorling Kindersley Limited and Editions Gallimard

This edition published in the United States in 2004
by DK Publishing, Inc., 375 Hudson Street, New York, NY 10014

04 05 06 07 08 10 9 8 7 6 5 4 3 2 1

A catalog record for this book is available from the Library of Congress.

ISBN 0-7566-0735-3 (HC) 0-7566-0734-5 (Library Binding)

Color reproduction by Colourscan, Singapore
Printed in China by Toppan Printing Co. (Shenzhen), Ltd.

Discover more at
www.dk.com

Lava stalagmite

Figure of Zhang Heng, Chinese seismologist

Contents

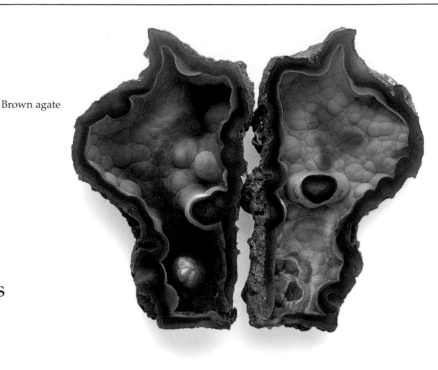

Brown agate

An unstable Earth

VOLCANOES AND EARTHQUAKES are nature run wild. An erupting volcano may bleed rivers of red-hot lava or spew great clouds of ash and gas into the atmosphere. During a severe earthquake, the ground can shake so violently that entire cities are reduced to rubble. Sometimes these disasters kill thousands of people, but most of the time they cause little damage to people or property. Volcanoes and earthquakes are natural events that happen all over the globe, though they are more frequent in some places than others. We think of volcanoes as cone-shaped mountains, but any hole through which lava reaches the Earth's surface is a volcano. Some are broad and flat, and most are found deep beneath the sea.

THE PERFECT VOLCANO
The graceful slopes of Mount Fujiyama in Japan rise 12,388 ft (3,776 m) above sea level. This dormant (sleeping) volcano is an almost perfect cone (pp. 38–39). According to Japanese legend, gods live at the summit (top), which is always shrouded in snow, and often in cloud. This view of the peak is one of a series of 36 prints by Katsushika Hokusai (1760–1849).

WALL PAINTING
Nearly 8,000 years old, this wall painting of an eruption of Hassan Dag in Turkey is the earliest known picture of a volcano. The houses of a town, Çatalhüyük, can be seen at the mountain's foot.

SAND TREATMENT
Eruptions may destroy homes and kill people, but they have their useful side. In Japan, "baths" in warm volcanic sand are believed to cure many illnesses.

ASHY VOLCANO
Ashy volcanic eruptions (pp. 14–15) are unpredictable, and observing them from the ground is dangerous. This computer-enhanced photo of Augustine volcano in Alaska was taken from the safety of a satellite. An ash cloud 7 miles (11 km) high is raining down on land and sea. Traces of it may travel around the Earth (pp. 34–35).

BACK FROM THE DEAD
Most of the people killed or injured in earthquakes are crushed when buildings collapse. This painting by the 14th-century artist Giotto shows a boy killed in a quake in Assisi, Italy. Legend has it that St. Francis of Assisi brought the boy back to life.

OLD FAITHFUL
Geysers are springs that shoot hot water and steam high into the air (pp. 36–37). They are formed when hot rock inside the earth warms groundwater. This geyser in Wyoming, Old Faithful, has erupted every hour for hundreds of years.

SPITTING FIRE
Mount Etna rises 11,122 ft (3,390 m) over the Italian island of Sicily, and is one of the highest mountains and most active volcanoes in Europe. Its barren summit is almost always bubbling with lava (left). Lava flows from a sizable eruption in 2001 destroyed ski-lift pylons, but stopped short of the village of Nicolisi. The nearby town of Catania is occasionally showered with ash from explosions.

SAN FRANCISCO, 1989
In 1906, San Francisco was flattened by an enormous earthquake. The shaking left large parts of the city in ruins, and the fires that followed added to the destruction. Earthquakes of this size seem to rock the area every hundred years or so. A smaller quake on October 17, 1989, shook many houses near the waterfront off their foundations. Some 62 people died in the 15 seconds of shaking.

Fire from below

A JOURNEY TO THE CENTER OF THE EARTH would produce quite a sweat. Only 25 miles (40 km) down in the Earth's crust (outermost layer), it is 1600°F (870°C) and the rocks are white-hot. Many metals melt long before they get this hot. But because of the intense pressure inside the Earth, the rocks, though soft, do not become molten (liquid) until much deeper. Most of the molten rock, or magma, erupted by volcanoes comes from the top of the mantle, the thick layer of rock between the Earth's crust and its core. Here pockets of magma collect as the Earth's penetrating heat melts the mantle rocks. Because magma is hotter and lighter than the surrounding rocks, it rises, melting some of the rocks it passes on the way. If the magma finds a way to the surface, it will erupt as lava.

TOO HOT TO HANDLE
The Irish artist James Barry painted this view of hell in 1788. In Christianity, hell is described as a fiery underworld where sinners are punished after death.

CHANNELS OF FIRE
The center of the Earth is hard to imagine. In this 17th-century engraving, Athanasius Kircher supposed a fiery core which fed all the volcanoes on the surface. We now know that because of extreme pressure, little of the planet's interior is liquid, and there are no underground connections between volcanoes.

Red-hot lava shoots out of a volcano in a curtain of fire.

INTO THE CRATER
Jules Verne's famous story *Journey to the Center of the Earth* begins with a perilous descent into the crater of Mount Etna. After many underground adventures the heroes resurface in a volcanic eruption in Iceland.

THIN-SKINNED
If the Earth was the size of an apple, the tectonic plates (pp. 10–13) that cover it would be no thicker than the apple's skin. Like the fruit, the planet has a core. This is surrounded by the mantle – the flesh of the apple.

BASALT
The ocean floors, which cover three quarters of the Earth's surface, are made of a dark, heavy rock called basalt.

GRANITE
The continents are made of a variety of rocks that are mostly lighter in weight and color than basalt. On average, their composition is similar to granite.

IRON HOT
Pure iron melts when it reaches 2,795°F (1,535°C). The Earth's inner core can be 13,000°F (7,000°C).

IRON HEART
The iron meteorites that fall to Earth are thought to be pieces of the cores of fragmented planets. Scientists believe the Earth's core is made of similar metals.

Crust, thicker under the continents than under the oceans

White-hot mantle of dense rock

Outer core of liquid metal

Inner core of solid metal

Ultramafic nodule

Ultramafic nodule

INNER SECRETS
No drill hole has ever reached as deep as the mantle. But occasionally, rising magma tears off fragments of the mantle on its way to the surface. Known as ultramafic nodules, these fragments of very heavy mantle rock are found in erupted lava flows. Their density and chemistry confirm present theories about the inside of the Earth.

LAYERS OF THE EARTH
Under the thin, relatively cool crust of the Earth lies the mantle. Made of silica and other metals, the mantle is solid, but contains pockets of magma that feed volcanoes on the surface. Beneath the mantle is the Earth's iron and nickel core, which has two parts. An outer core of liquid metal surrounds a smaller, solid inner core. The intense pressure in the inner core forces the metals to remain solid. At the surface the rock would be molten.

The world on a plate

VOLCANOES AND EARTHQUAKES are more common in some parts of the world than others. This was known early in the 19th century, but it was not until the 1960s, when the secrets of the deep ocean floor began to be revealed, that scientists found an explanation. This became known as the theory of plate tectonics. *Tectonic* is a Greek word that means "building". The tectonic theory says that the Earth's surface is fragmented into huge slabs called tectonic plates. These chunks of the Earth's crust move across its surface in response to forces and movements deep within the planet. The plate boundaries, where plates collide, grind past each other, or move apart, are areas of intense geological activity. Most volcanoes and earthquakes occur at these boundaries.

CONTINENTAL DRIFTER
German meteorologist Alfred Wegener (1880–1930) coined the term "continental drift." He saw how South America and Africa might fit together like puzzle pieces, and suggested that they had been attached. He guessed, incorrectly, that the continents drifted apart by plowing their way through the ocean floor. For over half a century his ideas were largely ignored by geologists. Only when mid-ocean ridges and sea floor spreading (pp. 24–25) were discovered was his theory accepted.

RING OF FIRE
There are more than 1,500 active volcanoes on Earth, and every year there are over a million earthquakes, mostly tiny tremors too small to be felt. On this map, the black cones are volcanoes and the red zones are prone to earthquakes. Both are common along the Ring of Fire, the edges of the plates that form the floor of the Pacific Ocean.

LESSONS OF HISTORY

This plaster cast shows a man killed in the eruption of Mount Vesuvius which devastated the Roman towns of Pompeii and Herculaneum in A.D. 79 (pp. 26–31). Eyewitness accounts of the time and recent excavations tell the horrific story of the eruption.

LIVING ON THE RING OF FIRE

In Japan, there are more than 70 active volcanoes, and few weeks go by without an earthquake or two. This huge quake in 1925 damaged the city of Kyoto.

Iceland sits on top of the Mid-Atlantic spreading ridge (pp. 24–25)

Kamchatka Peninsula is part of the Pacific Ring of Fire

Alaska and the Aleutian Islands have many volcanoes and earthquakes

The Mid-Atlantic Ridge is part of the largest mountain range in the world

The island of Réunion was formed by a hot spot (pp. 22–23) that was under India 30 million years ago

Antarctica is surrounded by new ocean made by mid-ocean ridges

Indonesia, home to over 125 active volcanoes, is at the boundary of several plates

DRIFTING PLATES

This globe has been colored to highlight some of the tectonic plates. A plate may contain both continent and ocean. The Australian Plate, for instance, includes a large part of the Indian Ocean. It is the plates, and not the continents, that are on the move.

Mount Erebus, an active volcano in Antarctica

There are no active volcanoes in Australia, which sits in the middle of a plate

Continued on next page

Moving plates

When tectonic plates meet, the great stresses of the shifting rocks are released in earthquakes. Most volcanoes also occur at plate boundaries, where magma forces its way through cracks in the plate and bursts to the surface. When two plates move apart, a mid-ocean spreading ridge – a chain of underwater volcanoes – is formed. When an oceanic plate collides with a continental plate, the lighter oceanic plate is forced beneath the other to form a subduction zone. The sinking plate partly melts, and the light magma rises to feed volcanoes just inside the plate boundary. Another kind of volcano erupts above a hot spot, an active center in the Earth's mantle.

FIRELAND
Fireland might be a better name for Iceland, a land of volcanoes and geysers (p. 7). The island is made almost entirely of volcanic rocks like those found on the deep ocean floor. It has gradually built up above sea level through intense and prolonged eruptions.

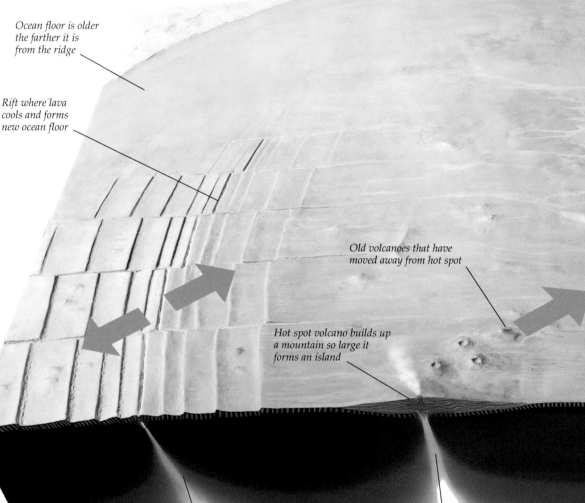

Ocean floor is older the farther it is from the ridge

Rift where lava cools and forms new ocean floor

Old volcanoes that have moved away from hot spot

Hot spot volcano builds up a mountain so large it forms an island

30 miles

60 miles

Hot mantle material rises, creating magma which erupts at the rift

Hot plume of magma rises to form a hot spot

The new plate is thicker in the cooler regions away from the heat of the ridge

MID-OCEAN RIDGES
New ocean floor is made where plates are moving apart (pp. 24–25). Here magma rises and solidifies, healing the gap between the plates. The continuous moving apart fractures the new plate material, causing small earthquakes. A series of ridges, each one older than the next, runs parallel to the central volcanic rift. All the ocean floor has been made this way in the last 200 million years.

HOT SPOTS
Hot spot volcanoes (pp. 22–23) are not found at plate margins. They are caused by active centers in the mantle which produce huge volumes of magma. The magma rises to the surface and punches a hole in the plate, forming a volcano. Because the hot spot in the mantle stays still while the plate moves over it, the hot spot seems to drift across the plate.

VOLCANO CHAIN
Guatemala in Central America is home to a chain of volcanoes, many still active. They sit on top of a subduction zone (see below) formed as the Cocos Plate sinks beneath the larger North American Plate.

AMERICA'S FAULT
The San Andreas fault zone is probably the most famous plate boundary in the world. It is easy to see the direction of movement from rivers, roads, and even whole mountain ranges that have been split apart by the relentless sideways sliding.

A deep ocean trench marks the region where ocean plates are subducted

Mountain range lifted where light oceanic plate rocks plunge into the denser mantle

There are few volcanoes along transcurrent plate margins

Ocean plate heated as it plunges into the mantle

Lightest melted rock rises through the surrounding dense rocks

Magma chamber feeds volcano

SUBDUCTION ZONE
Oceanic plate descends into the mantle in a subduction zone, causing earthquakes. As the crustal rock is "swallowed" by the mantle, the heat melts it to form magma. This rises with some molten mantle rock to feed volcanoes on the edges of the continental plate (pp. 14–15).

RUBBING SHOULDERS
A transcurrent plate margin is formed where two plates meet at an odd angle. The resulting boundary is called a fault zone. Large earthquakes occur when the fault sticks, then suddenly slips.

Lithosphere (crust and very top of mantle)

Asthenosphere (soft, upper part of mantle)

When a mountain explodes

SLUMBERING GIANT
Before the cataclysmic events of May 1980,
Mount St. Helens was a popular vacation spot
with tranquil forests and lakes.

THE MOST SPECTACULAR AND DESTRUCTIVE eruptions occur at volcanoes in subduction zones (pp. 12–13). These volcanoes may lie dormant for many centuries between eruptions (pp. 38–39). When they explode, the eruption can be extraordinarily violent. When Mount St. Helens in Washington State blew its top on May 18, 1980, it had been quiet for 123 years. The huge explosion that decapitated the mountain was heard in Vancouver, Canada, 200 miles (320 km) to the north. One side of the mountain was pulverized and blown out over the surrounding forest. This avalanche of rock was quickly overtaken by clouds of newly erupted ash. These became pyroclastic flows (p. 16) – flows of hot ash and gas that rushed down the steep slopes of the volcano at terrifying speeds, incinerating everything they met. The explosion continued for nine hours, spewing millions of tons of ash 15 miles (24 km) into the atmosphere. Mudflows (pp. 56–57) choked the river valleys with a mixture of ash, ice, and uprooted trees. Vast areas of forest were flattened by the blast and 62 people, including the volcanologist David Johnston, were killed.

THIRTY-EIGHT SECONDS AFTER THE FIRST EXPLOSION
After two months of small earthquakes and explosions, the north slope of Mount St. Helens had grown a huge bulge. At 8:32 A.M. on May 18, the whole north side suddenly gave way and slid down the mountain. As the pressure inside the volcano was reduced, the hot magma below began to froth and explode. This picture, taken 38 seconds into the explosion, shows the avalanche roaring down the north face. Just above the avalanche, a cloud of ash and gas is blasting skyward.

Ashy eruption cloud

Feeder pipe

Chamber of hot, gassy magma

FEEDING THE FURY
Lighter than the solid rock around it, hot magma had risen under Mount St. Helens. The magma was formed when an old oceanic plate was melted in the subduction zone off the coast (pp. 12–13). Magma had gathered in an underground pool, the magma chamber. It was then transported to the surface through a long tube called a feeder pipe.

FOUR SECONDS LATER...
The avalanche of old rock has been overtaken by the darker, growing cloud of ash, which contained newly erupted material. Gary Rosenquist, who took these pictures, said later that "the sight…was so overwhelming that I became dizzy and had to turn away to keep my balance." From his viewpoint 11 miles (18 km) away, he didn't hear a sound through the whole blast.

MOVING WALL OF ASH

As the ash cloud blasted out beyond the sides of the volcano, it became lighter than air and began to rise. Gary Rosenquist took this last picture before he ran for his car. "The turbulent cloud loomed behind us as we sped down Road 99," he wrote later. "We raced toward Randle as marble-sized mud balls flattened against the windshield. Minutes later it was completely dark. We groped through the choking ash cloud to safety."

LAST GASP

In the months after the big eruption, the diminishing pressure in the magma chamber pushed up thick, pasty lava. The sticky rock was squeezed out like toothpaste from a tube. It formed a bulging dome, which reached a height of 850 ft (260 m) in 1986. At one point, a spine of stiff lava grew out of the dome. Like the larger spine pushed up by Mount Pelée in 1902 (pp. 32–33), this eventually crumbled to a heap of lava fragments.

TREE-REMOVAL ZONE

Mature forests of trees up to 165 ft (50 m) tall were flattened by the blast of the eruption. Closest to the mountain, in the "tree-removal zone," the ground was scoured of virtually everything.

ELEVEN SECONDS LATER...

The avalanche of old rock has been completely overrun by the faster blast of ash. On the right, huge chunks of airborne rock can be seen clearly as they are catapulted out of the cloud.

Ash and dust

Lapilli, small bits of frothy lava

Ash, smaller pyroclastic fragments

Dust, the smallest, lightest lava fragments

THE MOST EXPLOSIVE VOLCANOES spit clouds of ash high into the sky. In an eruption, gases dissolved in magma escape with such force that they blast hot rock into billions of tiny pieces, creating ash. The resulting rock fragments are known as pyroclastics, meaning fire fragments. They range from solid lava blocks as big as houses (p. 18) to powdery dust so fine that it circles the globe as part of our atmosphere (pp. 34–35). Between these extremes are blobs of liquid magma called bombs, lapilli (Latin for "little stones"), and ash. Very powerful explosive eruptions can hurl huge blocks several miles from the volcano. But the biggest fragments usually land near the vent. In some eruptions, the pyroclastics form flows that can be extremely dangerous. Unlike lava flows, pyroclastic flows move swiftly, causing destruction within minutes. Many of the worst volcanic disasters have been caused by pyroclastic flows or pyroclastic surges, flows containing more hot gas than ash.

CONSTRUCTING A CONE
Mountains are built up as pyroclastics burst from the crater and settle layer upon layer on a volcano's slopes. Gassy fire-fountain eruptions build cinder cones of bombs and ash. These cinder cones are two of several in a crater in Maui, Hawaii (p. 22).

Prehistoric pyroclastic flow deposit near Naples, Italy

Fine-grained ash

Pumice bomb (p. 21)

Lithic (old lava) fragment

Detail of pyroclastic flow deposit from Naples

GLOWING AVALANCHES
If the erupted mixture of hot rocks and gas is heavier than air, it may flow downhill at more than 60 mph (100 kph). Such a pyroclastic flow (also called an ash flow or glowing avalanche) may flatten everything in its path. Equally destructive are pyroclastic surges, flows that contain more hot gas than ash. The residents of Pompeii (pp. 26–30) and St. Pierre (pp. 32–33) were killed by searing pyroclastic surges.

VOLCANO BIOGRAPHY
Frozen in a volcano's slopes is a detailed history of its past eruptions. The rock layers, formed as falling ash cooled and hardened, can be dated, and their textures and structures analyzed. The ash layers in this cross-section were erupted by a volcano in England about 500 million years ago.

Their fields buried in ash, farmers lead their water buffaloes to greener pastures.

Long night of the ash cloud

After lying dormant for 600 years, Mount Pinatubo in the Philippines began erupting in June 1991. Huge clouds of ash were thrown into the air, blocking out the sunlight for days. The airborne ash slowly settled, burying fields and villages for miles around. Over 330 ft (100 m) of ash lay in drifts on the upper slopes of the volcano. Torrential rains followed, causing mudflows that cascaded down the river valleys and swept away roads, bridges, and several villages (p. 56). At least 400 people were killed and another 400,000 were left homeless. With no gas masks to protect themselves from the gritty ash, many of the survivors developed pneumonia. And many survivors' eyes were badly inflamed by the ashy air.

BURIED CROPS
A thin fall of ash fertilizes the soil (pp. 40–41), but too much destroys crops. Without water to wash off the layer of powder, this corn is inedible. Whole harvests were lost in the heavy ash falls that followed the eruptions of Mount Pinatubo.

BREATHING EASY
Every step raises fine ash that fills the air. Covering the mouth and nose with a wet cloth helps to keep the throat and lungs clear.

Fiery rocks

VOLCANOES ERUPT red-hot lava. Sometimes the lava oozes gently from a hole in the ground. At other times it is thrown into the air in spectacular fire fountains. Either way, the lava flows off in rivers of hot rock that may spread out and cover many miles before they cool. Fire fountains and lava flows are common in Iceland (pp. 12, 24) and Hawaii (pp. 22–23). They are relatively predictable, because they have a fairly steady supply of magma from the mantle. But if the lava is less fluid and its supply is variable, explosions occur at irregular intervals as volcanic gas escapes from the magma. As the gas content changes, a volcano may switch without warning from one type of eruption to another. Explosions throw out bombs and blocks – chunks of flying lava that surround the vent. It is dangerous to get close to more explosive eruptions because the size and timing of the explosions vary.

REMELTED LAVA
Some of the gas dissolved in magma is lost when lava erupts and cools. This piece of cooled lava was remelted in a special oven. It became frothy, showing that it still contained a lot of its original gas.

Dense round bomb

A red crust of the mineral hematite covers this bomb thrown out by Mount Etna, in Sicily, Italy (pp. 6–7).

BOMBS AND BLOCKS
Bombs and blocks can be as big as houses or as small as tennis balls. Bombs are usually rounded; blocks are more dense and angular. Their shapes depend upon how molten and gassy the lava was during flight. Very liquid chunks of lava plop to the ground; denser, more solid chunks thud or shatter as they land. Both bombs and blocks leave long, fiery tracks when they are photographed at night.

Small, explosive eruption photographed at night on Mount Etna

A TWISTED TAIL
The odd twists and tails of many bombs are formed as lava spins through the air.

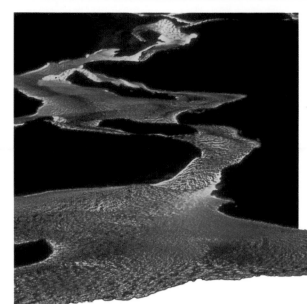

HAWAIIAN AA
Glowing red at night, the intense heat of an aa flow shows through the surface crust of cooling lava. Flows often advance in surges, piling lava higher and higher until it gives way and rushes downhill. Aa flows flatten most things in their path; thinner pahoehoe lava flows around trees and other obstacles.

PAHOEHOE FLOWS
Pahoehoe is more fluid than aa and contains more gas. As its surface cools, the flow grows a thin, pliable skin. The hot lava on the inside distorts the skin, wrinkling it so the surface looks like the coils of a rope. The crust may grow so thick that people can walk across it while red-hot lava continues to flow in a tunnel below (p. 23). The hot lava may remelt the overlying crust, which drips off. Kept hot by tunnels, pahoehoe lava can flow as far as villages on the volcano's lower slopes.

Hardened chunk of ropy pahoehoe lava

Aa and pahoehoe

Lava flows pose little danger to people, as they rarely travel faster than a few miles per hour. The two kinds of flows get their names from Hawaiian words. Aa (pronounced *ah-ah*) flows carry sharp, angular chunks of lava known as scoria. This makes them difficult and painful to walk over when they have cooled. Pahoehoe (*pa-hoy-hoy*) flows grow a smooth skin soon after they leave the vent and form ropy patterns as they cool. The skin traps gas, keeping flows beneath hot and mobile. Pahoehoe flows are rarely more than 3 ft (1 m) thick; the thickest aa flows may be 330 ft (100 m) high.

PAHOEHOE TOE
This picture shows red-hot pahoehoe bulging through a crack in its own skin. New skin is forming over the bulge. A pahoehoe flow creeps forward with thousands of little breakouts like this one.

Droplets of remelted lava from the roof of a pahoehoe tunnel

SPINY AND TWISTED
This chunk of scoria from the surface of an aa flow was twisted as it was carried along.

FIRE AND WATER
Volcanic islands like Hawaii and Iceland are usually fringed by black beaches. The sand is formed when hot lava hits the sea and is shattered into tiny, glassy particles. It is black because the lava is rich in dark minerals like iron oxides and low in light-colored ones like quartz.

Black sand from the volcanic island of Santorini in Greece

Gas and lightning

V OLCANIC GASES ARE DEADLY poisons. In August 1986, a small explosion in Lake Nyos in Cameroon, western Africa, signaled the release of a cloud of volcanic gases. The noxious fumes killed 1,700 people living in villages below the lake. The main killer in the cloud was carbon dioxide, a heavy gas which flowed downhill and gathered in valleys.

Captain Haddock and friends flee from a volcano's sulfurous gases in the Tintin adventure *Flight 714 for Sydney*.

Carbon dioxide is particularly dangerous because it has no smell and is difficult to detect – unlike many volcanic gases, which have strong odors. Hydrogen sulfide smells like rotten eggs, and the acid gases hydrogen chloride and sulfur dioxide sting the eyes and throat. They also eat through clothes, leaving holes with bleached halos around them. Poisonous hydrogen fluoride is strong enough to etch glass. Early volcano observers who thought they saw flames during eruptions were probably looking at great clouds of glowing gases. Flames occur when hydrogen gas catches fire as it leaves the vent. Even then, the flames are hard to see. More impressive are lightning flashes, which are often seen during ashy eruptions.

RAISING A STINK
Nearly 40 years after the last eruption of Kawah Idjen in Java, Indonesia, sulfur and other gases are still escaping into the volcano's crater. Here, volcanologist Katia Krafft (pp. 42–43) collects gas samples from the crater floor.

STEAM-ASSISTED ERUPTION
Water expands enormously when it turns to steam. So when red-hot magma meets water, the power of the eruption is greatly increased. When the new island of Surtsey was formed off Iceland in November 1963 (p. 41), seawater poured into the vent and hit the hot magma, producing spectacular explosions and huge clouds of steam.

GAS MASK
Made to protect the wearer against low concentrations of acid gases, this gas mask also keeps out all but the finest volcanic dust.

Volcanologists can study lava flows up close with the protection of a gas mask.

LIGHTNING FLASH
Immense flashes of lightning are often seen during eruptions. They are caused by a build-up of static electricity produced when the tiny fragments of lava in an ash cloud rub against each other. The electrical charge is released in bolts that leap through the cloud, as they do in a thunder-storm. This picture shows lightning bolts at Mount Tolbachik in Kamchatka, Siberia. It was taken during the day – the sun can be seen on the far left, shining feebly through a cloud of dust and gas.

VESUVIUS FLASHES
Lord Hamilton, British ambassador to Naples, saw lightning flashes as he watched the 1779 eruption of Mount Vesuvius (p. 31).

FLOATING ROCK
The volcanic rock pumice is light because it is full of bubbles of gas. If it has enough bubbles, pumice will float on water.

FLOATING ON AN ACID LAKE
Volcanologists sample volcanic gases on the surface of an acid lake in the crater of Kawah Idjen. The gases rising from the volcano are dissolved in the lake water that fills much of the crater. Acid lakes like this one are so toxic they can burn through human flesh in minutes.

Hot spots

THE LARGEST VOLCANOES ON EARTH are above hot spots.
Two of the biggest, Mauna Loa and Kilauea, are on the
island of Hawaii. The Hawaiian island chain is the tip
of a huge undersea mountain range that has built up
over millions of years as a stationary hot spot in the
mantle erupted great volumes of lava onto the moving
plate above it. Hot spots occur in the middle of plates,
not at plate boundaries, and most are beneath the oceans
(pp. 11–12). Geologists aren't sure how or why hot spots
form, but some believe that certain hot spots relate to old
plate boundary positions. Boundaries are marked by
fissures (cracks) through which magma can escape to the
surface. After an eruption, geological processes continue
in the mantle, and new magma eventually rises to feed
the hot spot. Other hot spots may be the beginnings of
new plate boundaries. Iceland is a hot spot 1,200 miles
(2,000 km) across. By creating new land through eruptions,
Iceland keeps northwestern Europe from being subducted
below sea level.

MAUNA LOA ERUPTS
During one of the longest eruptions
on Hawaii, Mauna Loa was active
at the same time as the younger
volcano Kilauea. Here fire
fountains have built a black
cinder cone (p. 16). Hot, quick-
moving pahoehoe lava (p. 19)
has overrun one side of the
cone, which has collapsed.

VOLCANO GODDESS
In Hawaiian legend, the powerful goddess
Pele makes mountains, melts rocks, destroys
forests, and builds new islands. The fiery
goddess is said to live in the crater
Halema'uma'u, at the summit of Kilauea
volcano on the island of Hawaii.

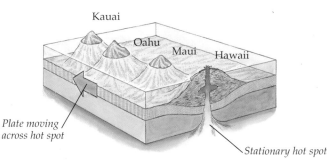

Kauai

Oahu

Maui

Hawaii

*Plate moving
across hot spot*

Stationary hot spot

A STRING OF ISLANDS
The Pacific Plate is moving over the stationary Hawaiian
hot spot, which is presently under the south end of the
island of Hawaii. There are two active volcanoes, Mauna
Loa and Kilauea, on Hawaii, and a third, Loihi, is growing
below the sea to the south. The north end of the island of
Hawaii is made up of older, extinct volcanoes, and a string
of progressively older volcanic islands lies to the northwest.

PELE'S HAIR
The hot, fluid lava of a Hawaiian fire fountain may be blown into fine, glassy strands. These are known as Pele's hair.

WANDERING HOT SPOT
Hot spot volcanoes erupt often and are relatively easy to get close to and photograph. This is Piton de la Fournaise on the island of Réunion in the Indian Ocean (p. 11). The island is the tip of a huge volcano that rises 4 miles (7 km) above the ocean floor. The hot spot has moved 2,500 miles (4,000 km) in the last 30 million years.

Lava has solidified around this tree, leaving a tree mold.

Road buried by lava during eruption of Kilauea

UP IN FLAMES
Lava in tubes remains hot and fluid, so it can travel many miles from the vent, engulfing fertile land and villages on the way.

LAVA TUBE
A pahoehoe flow may harden into a roof thick enough to walk on, yet only a yard or so below, hot lava continues to run in a tunnel, or tube. Occasional collapses in the roof provide a window through which the flowing lava can be observed. Hot lava dripping off the roof creates strange formations. Lava stalactites hang from the ceiling like icicles; stalagmites build upward from the tube floor.

Lava stalagmite made of drips in a pahoehoe tube

Sea floor spreading

Undersea volcanic mountain ranges called mid-ocean ridges occur on the ocean floor where two tectonic plates meet (pp. 10–13). Because of the huge pressure of the ocean water, these volcanoes erupt gently, squeezing lava out like toothpaste to form rounded shapes called pillow lava. The new rock fills in the widening gap, or rift, as the plates pull apart. Lava continues to erupt at the mid-ocean ridge, forming new ocean crust, while the moving plates carry older rock farther away from the ridge. This process is known as sea floor spreading. In this way the oceans grow about an inch wider per year. In places, the rifts bubble with black smokers – volcanic hot springs that shoot out water rich in metal sulfides. First discovered in 1977, black smokers are the subject of intense research. They are home to life forms found nowhere else on the planet.

RIFT THROUGH ICELAND
In Iceland, geologists can study ridges without getting wet. This is the Skaftar fissure, part of a 16 mile (27 km) long rift that opened in 1783, erupting 3.1 cubic miles (13 cubic km) of lava over eight months. The dust and gas killed 75 percent of the animals in Iceland, and 10,000 Icelanders died in the famine that followed.

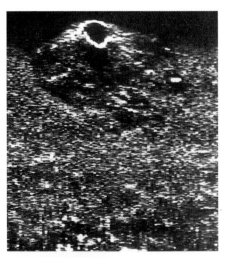

UNDERSEA VOLCANO
A kind of sonar called GLORIA used sound waves to create this image of a volcano 13,000 ft (4,000 m) below the Pacific Ocean. The volcano is 6 miles (10 km) across.

Icelandic eruptions give a glimpse of how mid-ocean ridges make new oceanic plate. The eruptions tend to be from long fissures, rather than central craters.

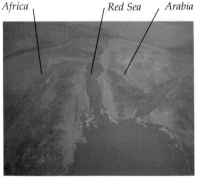

Africa   *Red Sea*   *Arabia*

SPLITTING CONTINENT
A mid-ocean ridge runs through the Red Sea. For the last 20 million years it has been making new ocean floor, as Arabia moves away from Africa.

Research submarine *Alvin* takes photos of mid-ocean ridges.

DEEP SEA SHRIMP
This new species of shrimp was found at the Galapagos rift in the Pacific Ocean in 1979.

Rounded pillow lava typical of lava erupted underwater

Black smokers

These hot springs are found along mid-ocean ridges in spots where sea floor spreading is great. The water black smokers spit out is hot, acidic, and black with sulfides of copper, lead, and zinc. These valuable metals come from the new oceanic plate that is formed at the ridges. The metals are dissolved by seawater flowing through the cooling rock.

Sulfur-eating tube worms from the Galapagos rift

MANGANESE NODULES
The ocean floor is carpeted with these black lumps rich in manganese and other metals. If a way of collecting them from such deep water can be found, they may become a valuable source of minerals.

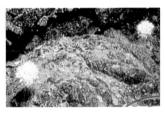

LIVING WITHOUT SUNLIGHT
The many unusual life forms found around black smokers are nourished by volcanic heat and minerals, particularly sulfur. These sea urchins were seen on the Galapagos rift.

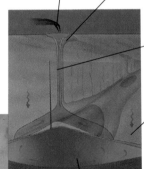

Plume of black metal sulfides

Black smoker chimney

Feeder pipe (p. 14)

Cold seawater passing through hot rock

Model of black smoker

Magma chamber

LAVA FEEDER PIPES
Two ancient lava feeder pipes can be seen in the rock above.

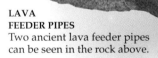

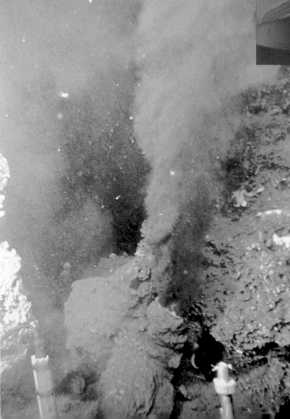

CHIMNEY PIPES
Chilled suddenly as they meet cold ocean water, the metal sulfides harden and crystallize to form the chimney pipes that surround the mouths of black smokers. These grow steadily, collapsing only when they get too tall.

Coarse crystal structure indicates slow cooling

Gabbro, a coarse-grained rock from an old sea floor magma chamber in the Mediterranean island Cyprus.

The great eruption of Vesuvius

PLINY THE YOUNGER
This scholar watched the eruption cloud from across the Bay of Naples, where he was staying with his uncle, Pliny the Elder.

PERHAPS THE MOST FAMOUS eruption of all time shook Mount Vesuvius near Naples, Italy in A.D. 79. When the long-dormant volcano erupted on August 24, the residents of the Roman towns of Pompeii and Herculaneum were taken by surprise. Hot ash and lapilli (p. 16) rained down on Pompeii for hours until it was buried several yards deep. Many people escaped, coughing and stumbling through the darkness of the ash cloud. Those caught in the town were overwhelmed by a sudden powerful blast of gas and ash (a pyroclastic surge, p. 16). The apocalyptic events were described in detail by Pliny the Younger. His famous letters to Tacitus are the first known eyewitness account of a volcanic eruption. The buried towns were virtually forgotten until excavations began in the 18th century. The digs have since unearthed a priceless archeological and geological treasure: two thriving Roman towns frozen in the moments of their destruction.

BLOWING IN THE WIND
The wind blew Vesuvius's ash cloud south onto the town of Pompeii. Herculaneum, to the west of the volcano, was hardly touched by falling ash. But the pyroclastic flows and surges (p. 16) that followed flowed downhill in all directions, covering both towns.

BURNT TO A CRISP
This carbonized loaf of bread was one of several found in the brick oven of a bakery. The baker's stamp can still be seen, nearly 2,000 years after the day the bread was baked.

BEWARE OF DOG
This Pompeiian floor mosaic (picture made of tiles) was meant to scare intruders. A similar mosaic says *cave canem* – Latin for "beware of the dog."

Modern Italian bread

Flour mill made of lava, a tough rock also used to pave streets

Portrait of a poetess or princess, from a floor mosaic found at Pompeii

Bowl of petrified eggs

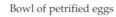

Fresh figs, still grown on the slopes of Vesuvius

SNAKE CHARM
Fine gold and silver jewelry, some set with emeralds, was found in Pompeii. This hollow bracelet in the shape of a coiled snake is made of thick gold. Certain styles were common. Over 80 copies of one kind of earring were found, suggesting mass production of popular models.

Fresh walnuts

Bowl of carbonized figs

Carbonized food

Wood, bone, most foods, and many other substances contain carbon. Normally these burn when heated. But in some circumstances, hot ash and gas prevent oxygen from combining with carbon, and carbon compounds are partially charred or turned to charcoal. This process, called carbonization, perfectly preserved the details of many foods in the fine ash at Pompeii.

Bowl of carbonized walnuts

PANIC IN THE STREETS
The large theater (the open, semi-circular building) and the gladiator's gymnasium (in front of the theater) can be seen in this artist's impression of the destruction of Pompeii. In the crowded streets, people are running for their lives from the menacing black clouds.

DEATH OF PLINY THE ELDER
In one letter, Pliny the Younger wrote of his uncle and another official fleeing with "pillows tied upon their heads with napkins; and this was their whole defense against the storm of stones that fell around them. It was now day everywhere else, but there a deeper darkness prevailed than in the thickest night…my uncle…raised himself up with the assistance of two of his servants, and instantly fell down dead; suffocated, as I conjecture, by some gross and noxious vapor…his body was found entire…looking more like a man asleep than dead."

Continued on next page

Continued from previous page

THE FAITHFUL DOG
This guard dog found at the house of Vesonius Primus died at his post, still wearing his bronze collar and chain.

Caught in the act of dying

Over 2,000 people died in Pompeii when the eruption of Mount Vesuvius destroyed the Roman town. We know about these Roman citizens from plaster casts that show them at the moment of death. As the fleeing Pompeiians died, the rain of ash and pumice hardened around their bodies like wet cement. Over time, the soft body parts decayed and the ash and pumice turned to solid rock. The shapes of the dead bodies were left as hollows in the rock. Only the hard bones remained inside the hollows. In 1860, the king of Italy appointed Giuseppe Fiorelli as director of the excavations. Fiorelli started the first systematic, large-scale digs of the ancient city. He also invented a method for removing the skeletons from the body hollows and filling the space with wet plaster of Paris. After the plaster hardened, a true representation of the bodies could be dug out of the volcanic rock. Many of these startling casts show people grimacing, trying to hide, or huddling together in terror. Excavations at Pompeii continue today, and Fiorelli's method is still used whenever new bodies are unearthed. The technique has also been used to make casts of animals, trees, doors, furniture, and the wheels of carts.

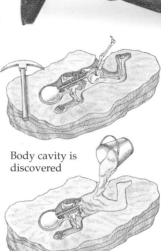

Body cavity is discovered

Cavity is filled with wet plaster of Paris

LAST DAY OF POMPEII
Fascinated by the apocalyptic stories of Pompeii, many artists have depicted its destruction. Like most, this painting by 19th-century German artist Karl Bruillov is rather fanciful. He has shown flames as buildings catch fire.

Cast of suffocated baby, found in the Garden of the Fugitives, where many fleeing Pompeiians perished

SHROUD OF DEATH
This body cast shows the folds of the clothing this man was wearing when he died. He is clutching his chest, indicating his pain in breathing. Most of the victims are believed to have died of suffocation.

Cast of man who died shielding
his face with his hands

*Part of
woman's
skull shows
through cast*

**KILLED
ON DUTY**
When the
American writer
Mark Twain visited
Pompeii, he was
impressed by the remains of
a soldier who had stayed
at his post "till the hell
that raged around him
burned out the
dauntless spirit it
could not
conquer."

MOTHER AND CHILD
This mother was trying to
protect her child when they were
overcome by the searing ash and
gas. They were found together
with several other families in the
Garden of the Fugitives.

*Pyroclastic
flow deposit*

*Pyroclastic
surge deposits*

Ash and lapilli

ROCK LAYERS
Pompeii was
buried by 6 ft
(2 m) of ash and
lapilli, then two
pyroclastic
surges and a
pyroclastic flow.

HEALTH WARNING
This skeleton mosaic found near Pompeii is a
memento mori, a reminder of death. The figure is
carrying wine jugs, perhaps to warn Romans of
the dangers of drinking alcohol.

Fiorelli takes detailed notes while
supervising an excavation

Continued on next page

Herculaneum

In A.D. 79, the Roman town of Herculaneum was a luxurious seaside resort. When Mount Vesuvius began to erupt on August 24, the great ash cloud that engulfed Pompeii (p. 26) missed Herculaneum. Less than 1 inch (3 cm) of debris had fallen on the town when it was blasted by a great surge of hot ash and gas. Early excavations uncovered very few bodies, which was puzzling. Archeologists decided that most of the inhabitants must have escaped in boats before the surge. But in the 1980s, several hundred skeletons were found huddled beneath massive brick arches that once stood on the shoreline. A great crowd of people must have taken shelter there, only to be overcome by the deadly waves of ash and gas.

NEPTUNE AND AMPHITRITE
This mosaic of two mythological figures was unearthed in the courtyard of a wealthy wine merchant's house in Herculaneum.

WALKING IN THE RUINS
The excavations of this Roman town have created a deep hole that is surrounded by the modern city of Herculaneum (p. 60). These visitors to the ruins are walking on a street paved with lava stones.

ROMAN SKELETONS
Unlike the bones found in Pompeii, the skeletons from Herculaneum have no surrounding body shape. Because Herculaneum was close to sea level, the volcanic ash became wet. As the bodies decayed, the wet ash was packed tightly around the bones.

A TOMB OF HOT ROCK
Herculaneum was hit by six pyroclastic surges (pp. 16–17). Each one was followed by a thick flow of hot ash, pumice, and rock. The flows buried the town in 65 ft (20 m) of volcanic debris – five times more than covered the neighboring town of Pompeii.

TEXT BOOK ERUPTION
This 1767 engraving (above), which probably shows the 1760 eruption, was published in *Millar's New Complete & Universal System of Geography.*

1631 eruption (left)

HAMILTON'S VIEW
The British ambassador to Naples, Lord Hamilton (p. 21), included this view of the 1779 eruption in his book *The Campi Phlegraei* (which literally means "flaming fields"). The artist is Pietro Fabris (p. 39).

The world's most visited volcano

The Romans who lived in the shadow of Vesuvius were scarcely aware that it was a volcano. The mountain had erupted 800 years earlier, but it had been calm since, and its slopes had grown green and peaceful. Vesuvius was more explosive after A.D. 79, erupting numerous times in the 20 centuries since Pompeii and Herculaneum were destroyed. The biggest recent eruption, in 1631, produced pyroclastic surges and flows. Since the 18th century, travelers have flocked to Naples to see the excavations, the art treasures, and the famous mountain. Even today tourists make the difficult climb to the summit and pay to look into the steaming crater.

German etching of 1885 eruption showing fires started by lava flows

ON THE TOURIST MAP
This cartoon shows English tourists at the crater of Vesuvius in 1890. A tourist guidebook of 1883 warns visitors that all guides are impostors. It advises sightseers to wear their worst clothes because boots are ruined by the sharp lava and colorful dresses are stained by the sulfur.

Vesuv. Ash rain of the eruption (March 1944: days 22. 23. 24. 25. 26)

TRAVELING IN STYLE
From 1890 to 1944, a steep cable railway carried sightseers up to the crater of Vesuvius. Here tourists watch the 1933 eruption.

SOUVENIR OF VESUVIUS
Centuries ago, souvenirs from Naples included Roman artifacts stolen from the excavations. These days security is tighter, and boxes of lava and ash are more common souvenirs. Guidebooks should warn that some boxes contain colorful industrial waste rocks instead!

A modern Pompeii: St. Pierre

ONE OF THE WORST VOLCANIC DISASTERS of the 20th century happened on May 8, 1902, on the French Caribbean island of Martinique. Mount Pelée, the volcano that towered over the city of St. Pierre, erupted just before 8:00 A.M., engulfing the city and all its inhabitants in a cloud of glowing gas. Many died in the cathedral where mass for Ascension Day, a Christian holy day, had just begun. Eyewitnesses on ships in the harbor described the cloud as shriveling and incinerating everything it touched. One said "the wave of fire was on us and over us like a lightning flash. It sounded like thousands of cannon." Within minutes, St. Pierre was charred beyond recognition. A thin blanket of ash coated the blasted remains of the city. A few sailors survived on their ships, but all but two of the 29,000 residents were killed.

Broken statuette

SCARRED SURVIVOR
The heat pitted the surface of this statue. Like many objects, it shows more intense heating on the side facing the volcano – in this case the back side.

ALFRED LACROIX
French volcanologist Alfred Lacroix arrived in St. Pierre on June 23, 1902, and spent a year studying Mount Pelée. In his famous report on the eruption, he described the strange "glowing clouds" that overran St. Pierre. Nowadays these would be called pyroclastic surges (p. 16).

Melted medicine bottle

WHEN THE CLOCKS STOPPED
This pocket watch was melted to a standstill at 8:15 A.M.

Carbonized spaghetti

Carbonized prune

Ash fragment

Remains of mousetrap

MELTED GLASS
Like the excavations of Pompeii, the ruins of St. Pierre still reveal secrets of the catastrophe. Discovered in the 1950s, these partially melted objects bear witness to everyday life in a small French colony at the beginning of the 20th century. Some are either so melted or so unfamiliar that it is hard to guess what they are.

Fine volcanic ash melted into glaze

Melted wine bottle

Melted metal fork (rust occurred after eruption)

Top of charred human femur (thighbone)

RUINED CITY
The walls of some buildings were all that was left standing in St. Pierre. During the eruption, rum distilleries and warehouses exploded in the heat, adding to the destruction.

Heap of glass melted beyond recognition

PROTECTING ANGEL?
This angel figurine, made of corroded metal, is barely recognizable. Unlike Pompeii and Herculaneum, no great works of art have been uncovered in St. Pierre.

Charred mug

Squashed candlestick

CARBONIZATION
Wood, bone, ceramics, and most foods contain carbon. When objects containing carbon are charred, they take on different forms, and sometimes are no longer recognizable. This process is known as carbonization (pp. 26–27).

Carbonized coffee beans

HOT ENOUGH TO MELT METAL
Some metal objects melted or partly melted. These iron nails were fused together. The metal spoon lost the tip of its bowl, where the metal was thinnest. The candlestick was squashed, probably when the building it was in collapsed (it shows little sign of melting). Copper telephone wires in the town were not melted, so the cloud must have been a little less than 1,981°F (1,083°C), the melting point of copper.

Pile of fused iron nails

Melted metal spoon

ETERNAL FIGURE
The wooden cross was burned right off this crucifix, leaving the figure of Jesus with outstretched arms.

Fused coins

OUT OF THE FRYING PAN
One of the two people left alive in St. Pierre was Auguste Ciparis. A prisoner condemned to death, he survived because his cell had thick walls with one tiny window that faced away from the volcano. He was later pardoned, and toured the world as part of a circus act under the name of Ludger Sylbaris.

Affecting the world's weather

A POWERFUL ASHY ERUPTION can have a dramatic effect on the weather. Dark days, severe winds, and heavy falls of rain or mud may plague the local area for months. If the gas and dust are carried high into the atmosphere, they may travel great distances around the globe. When this happens, the climate of the whole planet can be altered. The volcanic material filters out some sunlight, reducing temperatures on Earth. The particles also affect our views of the sun and moon by scattering certain kinds of sunlight and letting other kinds through the atmosphere. This can cause spectacular sunrises and sunsets. The sun and moon may seem to be wrapped in halos or to glow with strange colors. Two big eruptions in 1783 caused unusually thick polar ice to form, creating problems for explorers. In the longer term, volcanic particles may cause global cooling, mass extinctions, or even ice ages.

EARLY EARTH
About 4 billion years ago, planet Earth had no atmosphere and its surface was covered with erupting volcanoes. All the water in the oceans and many of the gases that make up the atmosphere have been produced by volcanoes erupting over the millennia.

LITTLE ICE AGE
Two major eruptions in 1783 – Skaftar in Iceland (p. 24) and Mount Asama in Japan – were followed by several very cold winters in Europe and America.

VOLCANIC SUNSETS
In A.D. 186, the Chinese noted unusually red sunrises and sunsets. These were caused by volcanic emissions from the huge eruption of Mount Taupo in New Zealand. This sunset was caused by dust from the 1980 eruption of nearby Mount St. Helens.

WHO KILLED T. REX?
The extinction of the dinosaurs remains a mystery. One theory proposes that massive volcanic eruptions changed the climate, creating bitterly cold weather. Another theory favors a climate change caused by an asteroid or comet striking our planet.

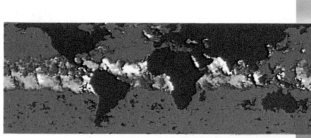

FLOATING AROUND THE GLOBE
The June 1991 eruptions of Mount Pinatubo in the Philippines (right and p. 17) spewed ash and gas into the atmosphere. Satellite images (above) showed that by July 25, the particles had spread around the world.

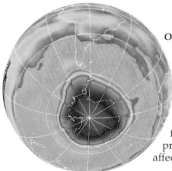

OZONE HOLE
This computer-enhanced satellite image shows the hole in the ozone layer over the Antarctic. The sulfur particles that Pinatubo threw high into the atmosphere may cause further damage to this protective layer. This could affect world temperatures.

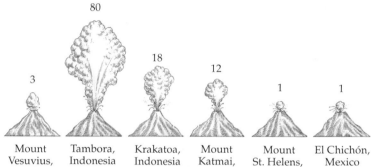

3	80	18	12	1	1
Mount Vesuvius, Italy A.D. 79	Tambora, Indonesia 1815	Krakatoa, Indonesia 1883	Mount Katmai, Alaska 1912	Mount St. Helens, Washington 1980	El Chichón, Mexico 1982

COMPARING THE SIZE OF ERUPTIONS
The amount of ash a volcano emits is a good measure of the size of the eruption. This diagram compares total emissions of six major eruptions. The units are cubic km (one cubic mile equals about 4.2 cubic km). Some large eruptions are relatively unknown. Mount Katmai covered remote parts of Alaska with huge quantities of ash in 1912, and the massive Tambora eruption of 1815 killed more than 90,000 Indonesians.

An artist's impression of the 1883 eruption of Krakatoa, Indonesia

ONCE IN A BLUE MOON
In 1883, the Indonesian island of Krakatoa was blown to pieces in a cataclysmic eruption (p. 57). The explosion, one of the loudest ever recorded, was heard 2,400 miles (4,000 km) away at Alice Springs, Australia. Dust and gas colored sunsets in Europe, where the moon and the sun appeared to be blue or green. Floating islands of pumice drifted in the Indian Ocean for months afterward, causing a great hazard to ships. This piece of pumice was washed up on a beach in Madagascar, 4,200 miles (7,000 km) away.

35

Steam vents and boiling mud

WHERE VOLCANIC HEAT WARMS an area, the water in the ground is heated too. When volcanoes are dormant (sleeping) for long periods, this hot water may shoot to the surface in geysers (p. 7), steam vents, hot springs, and pools of bubbling mud. These hydrothermal (hot-water) features make for spectacular scenery in places as far apart as Japan, New Zealand, Iceland, Italy, and the United States. The hot water can also be harnessed to do useful work, if it is not too acidic and its flow is constant. Steam can be directed to spin turbines and generate electricity. In Iceland, hot groundwater is piped into cities where it is used to heat homes and greenhouses. Many active volcanoes also release steam and other gases between eruptions. Changes in their gas emissions may help us predict future eruptions.

VULCAN, GOD OF FIRE
The ancient Romans believed Solfatara volcano near Naples, Italy, was an entrance to the underworld. It was also one of the workshops of the blacksmith Vulcan, the god of fire, for whom volcanoes are named.

MEASURING THE EARTH'S HEAT
A thermocouple (p. 43) is being used to measure the heat of a fumarole (steam vent) in Solfatara crater. Temperatures here get up to 285°F (140°C). Monitoring changes in temperature also helps indicate which fumaroles might provide hydrothermal energy.

WORKING UP A SWEAT
The fumaroles in Solfatara release acid gases as well as steam. This observatory built in the 19th century is being eaten up by fumarole activity. Where the steam emerges in caverns or grottoes, it is believed to have miraculous healing powers. Since Roman times visitors have been taking steam baths to treat arthritis and breathing problems, or just to get the supposed benefits of a good sweat.

CRYSTALS OF SULFUR
The sulfur in volcanic gas cools and crystallizes. Under certain conditions, the yellow crystals of this non-metallic element grow large and translucent (partly transparent). These huge crystals are from Sicily, where sulfur has been mined for centuries. Sulfur has many uses, particularly in manufacturing. It is added to rubber to make it stronger in a process called vulcanization – named after the Roman fire god.

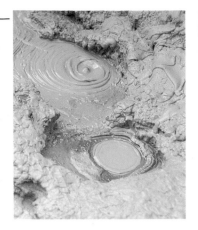

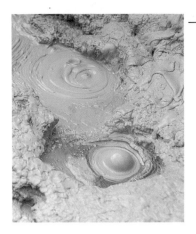

BUBBLING MUD

Some fumaroles bubble up through a mud bath of their own making. The acid sulfur gases corrode the rock they pass through, creating a great pool of soft mud. The bubbles burst at the surface with strange plopping sounds. The mud in this pot at Solfatara is 140°F (60°C). Some mud pots are much hotter; others are cool enough for people to soak in. Mud baths are popular beauty treatments used to soften the skin.

BAD BREATH

Spiky growths of sulfur crystals can be clearly seen around this fumarole vent. Close to the vent, the hot, rotten-smelling gases are invisible. Like the steam from a teakettle, the gases show up only when the water vapor begins to condense a few inches away.

ROMAN BATHS

The ancient Romans liked the luxury of hot, running water and built huge public baths. Baths fed by natural hot springs became medical centers where sick people came to bathe in the mineral-rich water. Many of these spa towns still flourish, and the ill travel great distances to come and "take the waters."

Crust of tiny sulfur crystals from fumarole in Java, Indonesia

Souvenir plate showing Old Faithful geyser, Wyoming (p. 7)

HOT-WATER POWER

About 40 percent of Iceland's electricity comes from hydrothermal power stations. As the technology improves, this figure is increasing, and other volcanically active countries like Japan, the United States, and New Zealand are developing their hydrothermal power programs.

Sleeping beauties

Church built on eroded remains of old volcano, Le Puy, France

Volcanoes are sometimes dormant for years or even centuries between eruptions. During this period of rest, volcanic gases may seep quietly from the cooling magma that lies beneath the volcano. As these gases rise through the rocks of the volcano, they react chemically with the minerals already in the rocks to create new minerals. These are often brightly colored with large crystals. At the Earth's surface, the gases rise into the atmosphere. The crater left at the end of the last eruption gradually weathers. Vegetation grows over the new rocks (pp. 40–41), and erosion by wind and water makes slopes less steep. If the period of dormancy is tens of thousands of years, it may be difficult to recognize that a volcano ever existed. At that stage it may at last be safe to assume that the volcano is extinct.

Radiating zeolite crystals from the Faeroe Islands

BORN IN THE LAVA
Zeolite crystals grow in old gas bubbles in lava. They are found in a great variety of shapes and colors.

AGATES
These beautiful banded stones form in cavities (hollow spaces) in cooled or cooling volcanic rocks. Each band is formed at a different time, and is colored by combinations of oxygen and iron.

Outer layers of this agate are oldest

Adventurers descend into the crater of Hekla, Iceland, in 1868

CRATER LAKE
Craters often fill with rainwater between eruptions. This crater lake, on the volcano Shirane in Japan, is very acidic, due to gas seeping up from the magma chamber below and dissolving in the water (pp. 20–21). During an eruption, the acidic water may be hurled out of the crater. Mixed with hot rock and debris, it could race downhill in a deadly mudflow (pp. 56–57).

Brightly colored rocks seen at Solfatara (pp. 36–37) by Lord Hamilton and illustrated by Pietro Fabris

Cut diamond

Olivine from St. John's Island in the Red Sea

Forged in the fiery furnace

Hot volcanic fluids concentrate some unusual chemical elements. These cool slowly inside gas bubbles or other cavities in the volcanic rock. The slow crystallization produces large, perfectly-formed crystals, which can be cut and polished into gemstones. The harder stones are the most prized because they last forever. Diamond is the hardest stone of all. Softer stones are valued for their rich colors.

Cut peridot

RED SEA GEM
Gem-quality olivine is a deep green color. The gem is known as peridot.

Uncut diamond in volcanic rock from the mantle, from Kimberley, South Africa

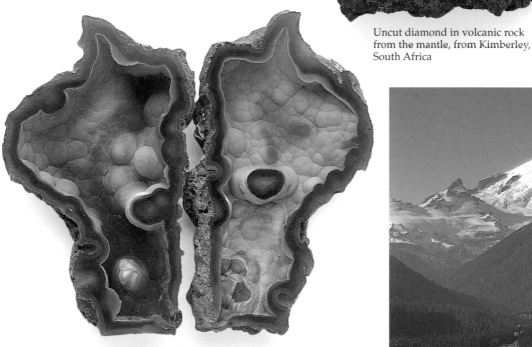

Agate-lined geode (cavity) from Brazil

BIRTH OF A CALDERA
During a large ashy eruption, the empty magma chamber may not be able to support the weight of the volcano's slopes. The slopes collapse inward, leaving a huge circular depression called a caldera. Calderas may be many miles across.

SANTORINI
This group of Greek islands is the top of a caldera formed by a huge volcanic eruption in 1645 B.C. The massive explosion may have led to the collapse of the Minoan civilization on the neighboring island of Crete. These events may even be the basis of the myth of Atlantis, an island said to have been destroyed in a fiery apocalypse.

CASCADE VOLCANO
Mount Rainier is one of a chain of volcanoes in the Cascade Range that includes Mount St. Helens (pp. 14–15). Any of them could become active again one day. There are no written records, but Mount Rainier probably erupted several times in the 19th century. These events have been dated from tree rings, which show a stunting of growth following an eruption.

Life returns to the lava

1944 lava flow, Mount Vesuvius

A VOLCANIC ERUPTION has a profound effect on the landscape. Around the world, land is a valuable resource where crops are grown to feed the population. For landowners and farmers, an eruption that produces less than 8 in (20 cm) of ash is a blessing. The ash is full of nutrients that enrich the soil. But too much free fertilizer is catastrophic. When the land is overrun by lava flows, farmland is unproductive. Thick flows can take months to cool. Decades, and in harsh climates even centuries, may pass while mosses and lichens spread slowly across the barren lava. Flowering plants and trees follow. The upper surface of the solid rock is slowly weathered, and the roots of the plants help break down the lava to form soil. Only when rich soil covers the land is it lush and fertile again. This process may take generations.

PUTTING DOWN ROOTS
A fern takes root in a ropy pahoehoe lava flow less than a year old on the slopes of Kilauea volcano, Hawaii (pp. 22–23).

Bare lava

Dense, interlocking crystal structure

A few lichens find a home on the lava

Lichen covers the lava, providing a soft surface for other organisms

GATHERING MOSS
How quickly lava is recolonized by plants depends on the nature of the erupted material. Ashy pyroclastic material is recolonized the fastest. Plants are slowest in taking root on lava flows. The climate and altitude are also important – plants return most quickly at low altitudes in the tropics. These pieces of lava are all from the same 1944 aa flow on the west slope of Mount Vesuvius in Italy. Almost 50 years later, lichen covers a lot of the flow, and moss, grasses, and weedy flowering plants are taking root. The only trees – small pines – were planted by the government.

Grasses, often the first flowering plants

Beginnings of topsoil

Lichen cling to exposed parts of rock

Rock breaks down to soil, and grass and moss take root

Moss grows in thin soil

New cone is still bare ash

Monte Somma, part of caldera (p. 39) left by huge, prehistoric eruption

Pine forests cover lower slopes

Mount Vesuvius steaming after mild eruption of 1855

BIRTH OF AN ISLAND
In November 1963, an undersea eruption off the southwest coast of Iceland gave birth to a new island, Surtsey (p. 20). On the third day (above), eruptions were still highly explosive.

WASHED ASHORE
Seeds blown by the wind or washed up on the beach of Surtsey soon took root in nearby ash fields (above). The beach itself was too harsh for most plants to live on.

THROUGH THE GRAPEVINE
The lush land around Vesuvius has been fertilized by ash from regular eruptions over the last 20 centuries. The ash supports a large grape harvest, which in turn supports the local wine industry.

LACHRIMA CHRISTI
Mount Vesuvius is featured on the label of this wine made from grapes grown on the volcano's slopes. Without the potassium, phosphorus, and other plant nutrients that the volcanic ash brings to the fields, the vines would not grow so thickly and the wine would taste less sweet.

Peacock butterfly lives on nectar of flowering plants

Weedy flowering plant

Eventually, soil cover is thick enough to support larger plants.

ROMAN AMPHORAE
The stacks of amphorae jugs for storing wine and olive oil found at Pompeii (pp. 26–31), are evidence of how fertile the soil was in Roman times.

FLOWER OF LYDIA
This brilliantly colored shrub is one of the first plants to grow on the lava at Vesuvius.

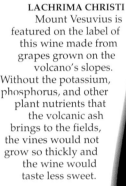

Mosaic of Venus, Roman goddess of fertility, from Pompeii

Being a volcanologist

FOR A VOLCANOLOGIST – a scientist who watches, records, and interprets volcanoes – life can get uncomfortably hot. Volcanologists spend years monitoring volcanoes to try to predict when and how they will next erupt. Most of their time is spent analyzing data in an office or laboratory, but fieldwork on the slopes of active or erupting volcanoes is vital. This involves taking lava and gas samples and measuring changes in temperature and landforms – sometimes while having to wear protective clothing. Hopes of accurate predictions rose in the early 2000s, when scientists identified vibrations, or tremors, lasting a minute or more. They occur when magma forces its way upward through cracks inside the volcano. As their frequency increases, scientists hope to be able to predict the time of an eruption.

KATIA KRAFFT
French volcanologists Katia and Maurice Krafft devoted their lives to documenting volcanoes. This photo taken by Maurice shows Katia observing a fire fountain in a protective suit. The husband-and-wife team were killed during the eruption of Mount Unzen in Japan in 1991.

SPACED-OUT SUIT
This protective suit has a metal coating that reflects the intense heat of a volcanic eruption and leaves the scientist inside cool. But it also inhibits the wearer from feeling, hearing, or seeing what is going on. In a tight spot, the bulky suit may stop him or her from running to safety.

VOLCANO BIOGRAPHY
The volcanologist's notebook is the history of a volcano, like a chapter from its biography. The observer makes notes and sketches of all the big (and little) events during an eruption. The significance of some things may only become clear later.

HOT ROD

This metal rod is ideal for collecting red-hot lava. From relative safety at one end of the pole, the volcanologist dips the far end into the lava flow. He or she then twists it around, hooking up a blob of lava, which cools quickly once it is pulled out of the main flow.

Hard hat

Binoculars

TAPE MEASURE

A tape measure is handy to check up on cracks in the ground, which may widen unnoticeably from day to day.

Gloves made from the heat-resistant mineral asbestos

A CLOSER LOOK

Binoculars allow people to view a volcano close-up (in this case, Kilauea in Hawaii) from a safe distance.

TOO HOT TO HANDLE

To collect warm samples and work close to red-hot lava, volcanologists wear asbestos gloves. Hard hats protect against small volcanic bombs (pp. 16, 18).

Spirit level

PATHFINDER

The ground of an erupting volcano is continually changing as molten lava hardens into rock and builds new landforms. The mining transit is a surveying tool that is good for simple, rapid mapping. It has a compass and a spirit level (to find verticals and horizontals). Small and light, it can be clipped onto the volcanologist's belt.

Compass

Rotating stage

Thermometer reading up to 480°F (250°C)

MAPPING THE MOVING EARTH

A precise level can detect the small changes in ground level that foretell an eruption.

TAKING THE VOLCANO'S TEMPERATURE

Katia Krafft risks searing heat to take the temperature of a lava flow on Piton de la Fournaise volcano, Réunion (p. 23). She is using a kind of electric thermometer called a thermocouple; a glass thermometer would melt. The reading was 2,000°F (1,100°C), which is 760°F (300°C) less than the melting point of steel.

Folding, portable tripod

Volcanoes on other planets

SPACE EXPLORATION HAS SHOWN that volcanic activity is one of the most important geological processes in the solar system. The many space missions of the last two decades have brought back photographs and even rock samples from other planets. Some craft will never return to Earth, andwill travel into deep space, beaming back information, that can be translated by computers into detailed images of the more distant planets. We now know that many planetary bodies are scarred by huge craters. But few of these are volcanic. Most are impact craters, the scars left by collisions with meteorites. Like Earth, the moon, Venus, and Mars have solid surfaces that have been partly shaped by volcanic activity. The volcanoes on the moon and Mars have been extinct for millions of years. Scientists suspect that Venus's volcanoes may still be active. No other planets in our solar system have active volcanoes. But Io, one of Jupiter's 16 moons, shows volcanoes that are active and erupting.

TIDYING THE PLANET
The hero of Antoine de Saint-Exupéry's children's story *The Little Prince* lives on a planet (Asteroid B–612) with two active volcanoes. Before setting off on a journey, he cleans them out to be sure they won't erupt and make trouble while he's away; he knows this could happen if their throats get blocked and they cannot breathe. He also cleans out his one extinct volcano, because, as he says, "One never knows!"

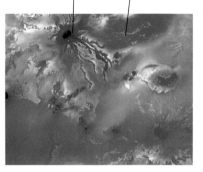

Crater probably contains liquid sulfur, which shows up dark

Sulfur flows

COLORFUL MOON
When the two *Voyager* spacecraft flew past Io in 1979, they revealed the most colorful world yet discovered in the solar system (other than Earth). Io's surface is spotted with red, yellow, orange, and brown, the colors sulfur turns as it slowly cools and solidifies.

OLYMPUS MONS
The extinct volcano Olympus Mons is 370 miles (600 km) across and rises 15 miles (25 km) above the surrounding plain. This makes it the highest point on Mars – and the largest volcano yet found in the universe, bigger than the entire Hawaiian island chain (pp. 22–23). Huge calderas (p. 39) nest one inside the other at its summit.

Clouds of ice shroud the summit

Sif Volcano

Gula Volcano

BENEATH THE CLOUDS
The spacecraft *Magellan* used imaging radar to penetrate the dense atmosphere of Venus. The images revealed huge volcanoes and impact craters beneath the clouds. Like most features on Venus, they were named after women, including goddesses from mythology.

ERUPTING INTO SPACE
One of the most exciting discoveries in the exploration of the solar system was the erupting volcano Prometheus on Io. Seen in this *Voyager* image, the volcano is spewing a plume of gases 100 miles (160 km) above the solid surface. The plume looks pale against the black of space. The eruption clouds shoot far into space because Io has very low gravity and virtually no atmosphere.

Vidicon camera viewer

SPACE VOYAGERS
The two *Voyagers* were launched in
1977. They flew past Jupiter in 1979
and Saturn in 1980–1981. This is a
model of *Voyager 1*, which headed
for the limits of our solar system
after passing Saturn. *Voyager 2*
flew by Uranus in 1986. In 1989,
12 years after its launch, *Voyager 2*
sent back data
from Neptune.

*190-mile
(300-km)
high gas
plume from
volcano Pele*

Lava flows

SHOOTING THE STARS
The two *Voyager* craft
caught eight of Io's volcanoes in the act of
erupting. They also saw about 200 huge calderas,
some filled with what seem to be active lava
lakes. Vidicon, a type of TV camera, uses an electron gun
and a photoconductor to collect the images. The
information is then transmitted back to Earth as a series
of pixcls – picture elements arranged in lines. These are
then processed and colored to create
simulated "photos."

*Dark,
inactive
volcano,
Babbar
Patera*

*Propulsion fuel
tank for making
delicate adjustments
to flight path*

When the earth moves

Cartoon about the San Francisco quake of 1906, captioned "I hope I never have one of those splitting headaches again."

Bᴇɪɴɢ ɪɴ ᴀ ʟᴀʀɢᴇ ᴇᴀʀᴛʜǫᴜᴀᴋᴇ is a terrifying experience. Earthquakes happen when the pressure between two tectonic plates (pp. 10–13) is so intense that the plates shift their positions suddenly, causing the earth to shake. When the shaking starts, there is no way of knowing how long it will go on or how severe it will be. The longest tremor ever recorded, the Alaskan earthquake of March 27, 1964, lasted four minutes (p. 57), but most quakes last less than a minute. In those brief moments, homes, stores, even entire cities are destroyed. The ground may appear to move like waves, and great cracks may open in the ground. Sometimes, despite powerful shaking, the rocks at the surface may not show any signs of the earthquake. For months after a quake people may feel unsettling aftershocks – small tremors that follow a major earthquake.

DISASTER MOVIE
This film about an earthquake destroying Los Angeles was shown in "Sensurround" – a low-frequency sound system meant to simulate earthquake shaking.

SHAKEN TO THE FOUNDATIONS
Almost 75 years old, these wood buildings in the Marina district of San Francisco had been built on a landfill site. They slipped off their foundations as the filled land settled in the shaking of the 1989 earthquake (p. 7).

PANIC SETS IN
People leave buildings and rush into the streets in panic as an earthquake shakes the city of Valparaiso, Chile, in 1906. Buildings are collapsing as their walls crumble.

FOLDED
This book was damaged in the earthquake which devastated Skopje, Yugoslavia, on July 26, 1963. It was found in the ruins of a collapsed building. Skopje sits on the same site as the ancient city of Scupi, which was completely flattened by an earthquake in A.D. 518.

ROCKING THE TEMPLE
The Roman towns of Pompeii and Herculaneum were rocked by a large earthquake in A.D. 62, 17 years before the huge eruption of Mount Vesuvius (pp. 26–31). A marble section from a house in Pompeii shows the tremor damaging the Temple of Jupiter.

Temple of Jupiter

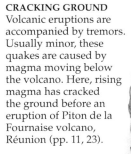

WHEN THE EARTH BREAKS
Solid rocks fracture to relieve the strain built up by the movement of tectonic plates (pp. 10–13). This road was cracked during an earthquake measuring 6.9 on the Richter scale (pp. 48-49).

SHAKEN UP
In *Natural Questions*, the Roman philosopher Seneca wrote about the earthquake that damaged Pompeii in A.D. 62. He was particularly interested in the psychological effects of the ground shaking and thought fear was a natural reaction. "Can anything seem adequately safe to anyone," he wondered, "if the world itself is shaken, and its most solid parts collapse?"

CRACKING GROUND
Volcanic eruptions are accompanied by tremors. Usually minor, these quakes are caused by magma moving below the volcano. Here, rising magma has cracked the ground before an eruption of Piton de la Fournaise volcano, Réunion (pp. 11, 23).

MOCKING THE SUPERSTITIOUS
The French writer Voltaire (1694–1778) wrote about the huge earthquake of 1755 in Lisbon, Portugal in his satirical novel *Candide*. The quake shocked Europe, and there were many theories about its cause. Voltaire made fun of religious figures who said God was punishing the city for its immorality. He also ridiculed residents who blamed – and then executed – several foreigners.

SOLID AS A ROCK?
This piece of limestone has a natural polish caused by earthquake stresses and strains. The flattened surface was almost melted by the frictional heat generated as the rock broke.

SHAKING, FIRE, AND FLOOD
The 1755 quake destroyed three quarters of Lisbon's buildings; fires that burned for six days afterward gutted most of the rest. Huge waves (*tsunamis*, pp. 56–57) destroyed the harbor, and were noticed as far away as England. More than 10,000 people died.

Intensity and magnitude

How do you measure the size of an earthquake? News reports usually rank the quake's magnitude (greatness in size) on the Richter scale. The Richter magnitude is useful because it can be determined from a seismogram – a recording of earthquake waves (pp. 52–55). The waves of a major quake can be recorded on the other side of the globe. As long as the distance between the recording device and the quake's center is taken into account, the Richter magnitude can be calculated from anywhere on the planet. But where the shaking is felt, it is more important to know how great it was and how it affected buildings and people. This is called the intensity of shaking. It is measured on other scales such as the Modified Mercalli Intensity Scale. Intensity is purely descriptive and cannot be recorded by a machine. It is compiled by inspecting the damage and asking survivors to fill out questionnaires. Every earthquake has just one Richter magnitude. But it has many intensities, which decrease away from the epicenter – the point on the Earth's surface directly above the quake's origin.

Giuseppe
Mercalli
(1850–1914)

Intensity

The Italian volcanologist Giuseppe Mercalli created his intensity scale in 1902. He used 12 grades with Roman numerals from I to XII. His scale was later updated to create the Modified Mercalli Intensity Scale.

I The shaking is not felt by people, but instruments record it.

II People at rest notice the shaking (above), especially if they are on the upper floors of buildings. Delicately suspended objects may swing.

III People indoors feel a vibration like the passing of a light truck. Hanging objects swing (above). Length of shaking can be estimated, but people may not recognize it as an earthquake.

IV Vibration like a heavy truck hitting a building. Dishes rattle; wooden walls creak; standing cars rock.

V Felt outdoors. Liquid in glasses splashes out (above); small objects knocked over. Doors swing open and close.

VI Felt by all. Many are frightened and rush outdoors. People walk unsteadily; windows, dishes break (above). Pictures fall off walls; small bells ring.

Magnitude

In California in the 1930s, Charles Richter compared the sizes of local earthquakes by using the tracings of the shaking which are recorded on seismographs (pp. 52–55). Knowing how far he was from each quake, he applied a distance factor to the maximum tracing. After allowing for the characteristics of the instrument, he came up with the quake's magnitude. Today, Richter's scale is used all over the world.

Charles F. Richter
(1900–1985)

RECORDING THE SHAKES
Richter took the smallest earthquake he could record at the time and called it magnitude 0. Today's instruments are much more sensitive, so the smallest quakes they register are given negative magnitudes. The highest Richter magnitudes recorded are about 9.

Grades of intensity for an earthquake that struck Japan on May 22, 1925

Epicenter

II III IV V VI

VII Difficult to stand (above). Furniture breaks; plaster and loose bricks crack and fall. Waves on ponds. Large bells ring.

VIII Driving becomes difficult. Walls, chimneys, monuments, steeples (above) often fall. Tree branches break. Changes in flow of wells and springs. Cracks in wet ground.

IX General panic. Animals run around in confusion. General damage to foundations of buildings. Frame buildings, if not bolted down, shift off their foundations (above). Underground pipes break.

X Most brick and frame buildings destroyed with their foundations (above). Some well-built wooden buildings destroyed. Large landslides. Water thrown out of rivers and canals.

XI Railway lines greatly distorted. Underground pipelines completely out of service. Highways useless. Ground distorted by large cracks. Many large landslides and rock falls.

XII Extensive damage. Nearly all built structures above and below ground destroyed or useless (above). Waves seen on ground surface. Objects thrown into air. River courses moved; surface dotted with cracks.

Waves of destruction

Earthquake waves travel rapidly, about 16,000 mph (25,000 kph) in rock, and more slowly in soft sand and mud. In the seconds after the plate movement that causes an earthquake, shock waves travel from the focus – the place inside the Earth where a quake begins. But sometimes the waves are slowed down and concentrated by soft sand and mud. This can cause severe shaking even far from the epicenter. The first waves to arrive are primary, or P, waves. They are fastest because they travel like sound waves, with a push-pull movement that causes little distortion in the rocks they pass through. The slower secondary, or S, waves are the next to arrive. They travel at slightly more than half the speed and distort the rocks in a more complicated sideways shearing movement. The slowest waves, surface waves, move in the most complex way. They often cause the greatest damage during an earthquake.

SEISMOGRAM
This is a recording of a 5.1 Richter magnitude quake. The time lag between the P and S waves – in this case, 17 seconds – is used to calculate the distance from the focus. The magnitude is calculated from the maximum P wave height, taking into account the distance and the sensitivity of the seismograph.

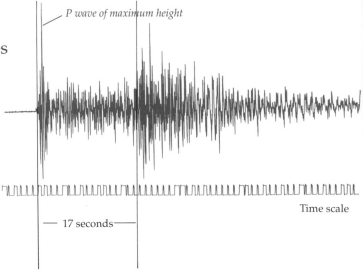

P wave of maximum height

Time scale

— 17 seconds —

First P wave   First S wave

Eskdalemuir, Scotland

Epicenter in Caspian Sea

Hyderabad, India

Lusaka, Zambia

Animals are restless, and may run around and cry

LOCATING AN EARTHQUAKE
On September 17, 1989, in Scotland, Africa, and India, seismologists – scientists who study earthquakes – recorded a quake of magnitude 6.1. All three stations calculated how far away it had occured and drew distance circles around the globe. The circles met in the Caspian Sea, identifying this spot as the epicenter of the quake.

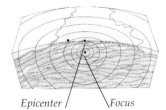

Epicenter   *Focus*

DEEP FOCUS
An earthquake's focus is usually many miles inside the Earth. From the focus, both P waves and S waves travel through the Earth to distant places on the surface. Surface waves begin at the epicenter and travel only on the surface.

Seismic station records first P waves

Church bells ring

People hear low rumbling like thunder

Startled by ripples, water birds fly off ponds

BEFORE THE EARTHQUAKE
Animals (and some people) may feel uncomfortable in the minutes before an earthquake strikes. They seem to sense that something is not quite right.

P waves

THE FIRST WAVES STRIKE
P waves, the first to arrive, may be so small that they are heard but not felt.

Woman sits by the ruins of her house in Lice, Turkey

DEVASTATED IN A MINUTE
The town of Pointe-à-Pitre on the Caribbean island of
Guadeloupe was shaken by an earthquake of Richter
magnitude 8 on February 8, 1843. Eyewitnesses said
the shaking lasted for about a minute. This was long
enough to reduce most of the buildings to ruins. A fire
that followed torched what was left of the town.

Living through an earthquake

This model shows the seismic (earthquake) waves from a
powerful quake as they pass through the countryside. The
epicenter is far off the page to the right. The fast P waves (in
yellow) have gone the farthest and are about to strike the area on
the far left. S waves (blue) follow, causing considerable damage.
The slowest waves, surface waves (red), arrive seconds later. They
have just reached the right of the model, where they have caused
the total collapse of buildings already weakened by the S waves.

*Trees and bushes
shake and rustle*

Ground cracks open

*Cracks appear
in buildings*

*Vehicles cannot follow
straight lines*

*Sand and water bubble out
of ground for hours after
shaking stops*

Fires start in ruins

Trees are uprooted

Landslide

People panic, have trouble standing up

Many buildings in ruins

S waves

SECONDARY WAVES STRIKE
The S waves follow the P waves. Here the
waves are shaking and distorting buildings
until they crack or collapse.

Surface waves

SURFACE WAVES
Some quakes generate powerful surface
waves that can cause serious damage far
from the epicenter.

Measuring earthquake waves

THE FIRST INSTRUMENT FOR RECORDING EARTHQUAKES was built by the Chinese scientist Chang Heng in the second century A.D. The original instrument did not survive, and we know of it only from descriptions of that time. It was a large bronze device about 6 ft (2 m) across. It was designed to record earthquakes too slight to be felt, and to tell roughly what direction the quake had come from. We now call it a seismoscope. In 1856, soon after the discovery of electricity, a more sophisticated earthquake recorder was invented. Built by the Italian Luigi Palmieri, it is a seismograph, a device that writes a permanent trace – known as a seismogram – of the earthquake shaking. It was also set up to measure the overall size of the earthquake shaking (pp. 48–49).

EARLY SEISMOLOGIST
The Chinese were keeping lists of earthquakes as early as 780 B.C. In the fourth century B.C., the Greek philosopher Aristotle suggested that tremors were caused by unstable vapors. But it was not until A.D. 132 that the Chinese geographer and astronomer Chang Heng (78–139) invented the first seismoscope.

Inner workings of Chang Heng's seismoscope

Pendulum

Suspension mechanism pulls on dragon's mouth

TOADS AND DRAGONS
Chang Heng's seismoscope is a bronze vessel ringed with dragons and toads. A heavy pendulum hangs inside. During a tremor, the vessel moves more than the heavy pendulum. This triggers one of the dragons to open its jaws. A bronze ball held there is released, and drops into the open mouth of the toad waiting below.

Ball held in dragon's mouth

The toad that is farthest from the epicenter catches the falling ball; this indicates which direction the quake came from

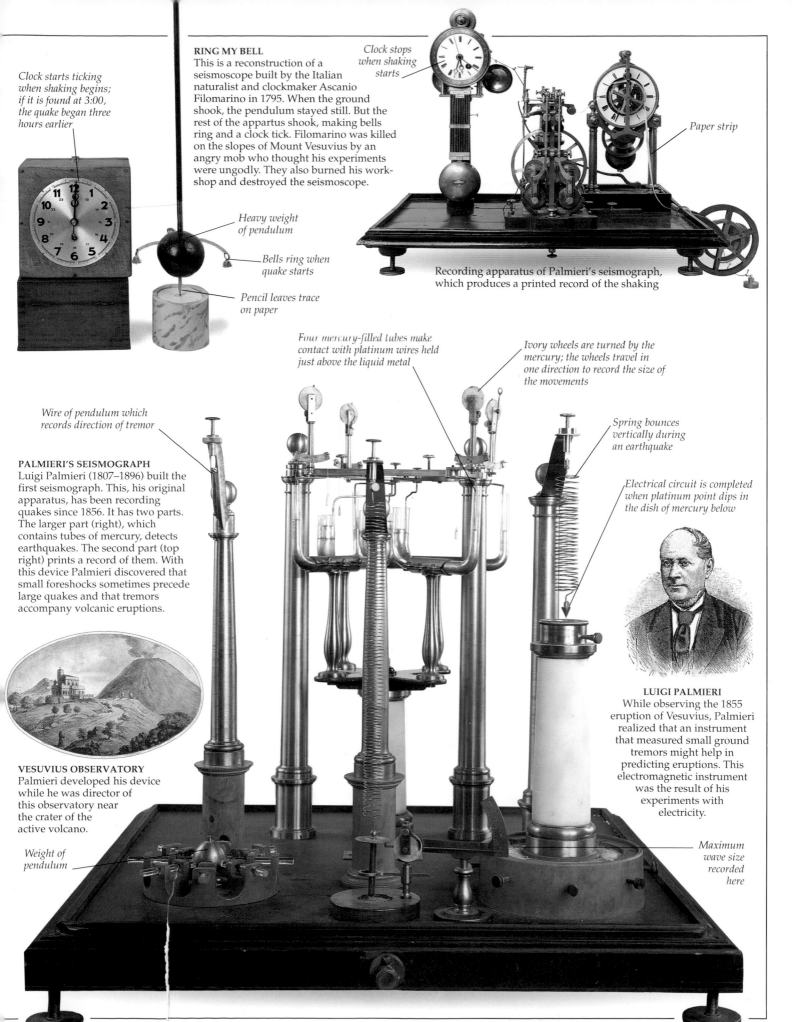

Clock starts ticking when shaking begins; if it is found at 3:00, the quake began three hours earlier

RING MY BELL

This is a reconstruction of a seismoscope built by the Italian naturalist and clockmaker Ascanio Filomarino in 1795. When the ground shook, the pendulum stayed still. But the rest of the appartus shook, making bells ring and a clock tick. Filomarino was killed on the slopes of Mount Vesuvius by an angry mob who thought his experiments were ungodly. They also burned his workshop and destroyed the seismoscope.

Clock stops when shaking starts

Paper strip

Heavy weight of pendulum

Bells ring when quake starts

Pencil leaves trace on paper

Recording apparatus of Palmieri's seismograph, which produces a printed record of the shaking

Four mercury-filled tubes make contact with platinum wires held just above the liquid metal

Ivory wheels are turned by the mercury; the wheels travel in one direction to record the size of the movements

Wire of pendulum which records direction of tremor

PALMIERI'S SEISMOGRAPH

Luigi Palmieri (1807–1896) built the first seismograph. This, his original apparatus, has been recording quakes since 1856. It has two parts. The larger part (right), which contains tubes of mercury, detects earthquakes. The second part (top right) prints a record of them. With this device Palmieri discovered that small foreshocks sometimes precede large quakes and that tremors accompany volcanic eruptions.

Spring bounces vertically during an earthquake

Electrical circuit is completed when platinum point dips in the dish of mercury below

LUIGI PALMIERI

While observing the 1855 eruption of Vesuvius, Palmieri realized that an instrument that measured small ground tremors might help in predicting eruptions. This electromagnetic instrument was the result of his experiments with electricity.

VESUVIUS OBSERVATORY

Palmieri developed his device while he was director of this observatory near the crater of the active volcano.

Weight of pendulum

Maximum wave size recorded here

Continued on next page

TOKYO, 1923
The city of Tokyo after the huge quake of 1923. Houses built of wood and paper were set on fire by overturned stoves. Thousands died in the fire storm that followed (p. 57).

Seismogram of 1923 Tokyo earthquake, recorded by Gray-Milne seismograph in Oxford, England

JOHN MILNE
An English geologist, John Milne (1850–1913), invented his own seismograph while he was teaching geology in Tokyo. He later set up the Seismological Society of Japan to study earthquakes.

Seismometers

Instruments that capture earthquake motion are called seismometers. They include a recording device, the seismograph, and produce a record, the seismogram. All seismometers work on the principle, developed by Chang Heng, that an earthquake shakes a heavy pendulum less than the surrounding ground.

Side view of Gray-Milne seismograph

Three pens write traces of vertical shaking and two kinds of horizontal shaking

One of two pendulums that registers horizontal shaking

Clock to indicate the moment quake starts

SHAKING AROUND THE CLOCK
This seismograph, designed in 1885 by the Englishmen Thomas Gray and John Milne, was the first meant for nonstop use. It had three pendulums and three pens, to record the three types of ground motion – vertical, east-west horizontal, and north-south horizontal.

A MODERN OBSERVATORY
At the new Vesuvius Observatory, great reels of paper record the ground movement measured by a series of seismometers set up at strategic points in the area. Many modern earthquake stations place their seismometers in remote places or in deep holes. Here they are far from confusing signals like heavy car or air traffic. Data is transmitted into the recording center by radio or along telephone lines. Modern seismographs record on magnetic tape, which allows for much better analysis.

PORTABLE
Networks of portable seismometers are used to monitor aftershocks of major quakes and ground tremors during volcanic eruptions. They were also used to prove that earthquakes did not cause the Lake Nyos disaster (p. 20).

MOONQUAKES
American astronauts left seismometers on the moon to record moonquakes. Many moonquakes are caused by meteorites hitting the surface. Others seem to take place most often when the moon is nearest to the Earth.

Case hides inverted, suspended pendulum

Paper drum winds very slowly between earthquakes; when shaking starts, gears change and drum starts feeding paper through much faster

Handle for winding up weight, which turns drum

Damping system, which ensures that each shock wave is recorded only once

Suspended weight drives paper drum (mechanical clocks driven in same way)

Smoked paper seismogram

Arm from which pendulums are suspended

HEAVY DUTY
This is a restored version of the seismograph invented by the German Emil Wiechert (1861–1928) in 1908. Its 440 lb (200 kg) mass measures the two horizontal types of ground shaking. It works along with a smaller instrument that measures vertical motion. The suspended pendulums are inverted (upside down), which makes them more sensitive. An even bigger Wiechert instrument has been operating at Uppsala in Sweden since 1904.

SMOKING UP
Early seismographs, many still in use, scratch their traces on smoked paper. This avoids the problems of ink, which can run out or glob – a disaster during tremors. The paper is smoked by coating it in the carbon produced by burning oil.

Mud, flood, and avalanche

THE TRAUMA OF AN EARTHQUAKE or volcanic eruption may have devastating aftereffects. Large ash eruptions are often followed by landslides or mudflows. The ash that piles up near the crater may collapse, bringing part of the mountain down with it. Heavy rains may combine with pyroclastic fragments to create a mudflow. In mountains, both quakes and eruptions may trigger avalanches; by or beneath the sea, both can cause giant water waves. These are incorrectly called "tidal waves", but they are not created by tides. Scientists prefer the Japanese name *tsunami*. Tsunamis may travel across oceans and pile up into walls of water as they approach the coast. When they break on faraway shores, they can cause horrendous damage.

SWEPT AWAY
The ashy eruptions of Mount Pinatubo in the Philippines (p. 17) were accompanied by mudflows that swept away roads, bridges, and several villages. The flows were caused by torrential rain falling on newly erupted ash.

Overview of Armero mudflow, 1985

BURIED IN A SEA OF MUD
In November 1985, an eruption of Ruiz volcano in Colombia, South America, spewed clouds of ash and pumice onto the snow and ice fields of the mountain's summit. This melted part of the snow, which in turn wet the ash, turning it into a flowing liquid. The heavy mudflow cascaded down the Lagunillas Canyon at speeds of up to 20 mph (35 kph). The city of Armero, 36 miles (60 km) away at the entrance of the canyon, was devastated by the roaring torrent of mud (left and below). About 22,000 people were buried alive by the flows of mud, rock, and debris that hardened around them like wet concrete. The only survivors were rescued from the edge of the flow (p. 58).

Truck trapped in mud, Armero

ABANDONED TOWN
Pozzuoli, near Naples, Italy, has been shaken by many small earthquakes. Part of the town was abandoned after shaking damage in 1983. The town has risen several yards since then, so the harbor had to be rebuilt lower down. Magma moving below the town is probably the cause of all these disturbances.

Old mooring post

New dock level

DWARFING FUJI
Japanese coastlines are plagued by tsunamis from both volcanic eruptions and earthquakes. The volcano Fujiyama (p. 6) can be seen in the background of *Giant Wave*, a picture of a tsunami by Katsushika Hokusai (1760–1849).

KRAKATOA, WEST OF JAVA
Tsunamis as high as 100 ft (30 m) crashed into surrounding islands after the cataclysmic eruption of Krakatoa (p. 35). The walls of water flattened many villages on Sumatra and Java (which is actually east of Krakatoa), killing 36,000 people.

ANCHORAGE
One of the largest and longest earthquakes ever recorded rocked Alaska on March 27, 1964. The shaking from the magnitude 8.5 quake lasted four minutes. It caused a layer of rock to liquefy under the sea cliffs of Turnagain Heights, a prosperous district of the city of Anchorage. Wooden houses wobbled like jelly as the ground sank beneath them and parts of the cliff slid into the sea. Most of the dwellings were left remarkably intact, tilted at crazy angles on the subsided ground.

AVALANCHE
Earthquake shaking may trigger avalanches that were just waiting to happen. In 1970, a magnitude 7.7 quake off the coast of Peru caused a disastrous slide of snow and rock which fell 13,200 ft (4,000 m) and killed over 50,000 people in the valley below.

FIRE IN THE RUINS
Firefighters douse a blaze after the 1989 San Francisco earthquake (p. 7). The fires that follow quakes or eruptions can burn cities to the ground. If gas mains are broken or flammable liquids spilled, the slightest spark causes fire. Shaking often damages the underground water supply, making a blaze harder to fight. The 1923 Tokyo quake (p. 54) was followed by a terrifying fire storm that swept through the city's wooden houses and left 200,000 dead.

State of emergency

THE CHAOS THAT FOLLOWS a big earthquake or volcanic eruption makes rescue difficult and dangerous. Many people may be killed by collapsing buildings in the few seconds the violent earthquake shaking lasts. More die from injuries in the next few hours. But people trapped in fallen debris may survive for days. For rescuers, finding them and getting them out is a race against time. It may be hard to rescue trapped people without putting more people at risk. Half-collapsed buildings may topple at any moment. Hazardous substances could suddenly catch fire or explode. In ash flow or mudflow eruptions, no one knows when to expect another surge. Damage to telephone lines, television and radio connections, and electricity, gas, and water supplies makes rescue operations even harder.

PERILOUS RESCUE
A survivor is lifted by helicopter from hardening mud in Armero, Colombia, in 1985 (p. 56).

MUDDY ESCAPE
An unconscious survivor is rescued from the mudflows that engulfed Armero in 1985. About 36 miles (60 km) from the volcano, parts of the mudflow were still hot, and survivors had to be treated for burns.

Controls showing level of infrared radiation

FINDING LIVE BODIES
A thermal image camera is used to locate people trapped after an earthquake. Wounded or unconscious survivors are often buried in the rubble of their collapsed homes. The camera uses infrared radiation to detect the heat of a living person. It is easiest to use the camera in early morning to avoid picking up the natural heat of other objects.

Strap worn around neck ensures that expensive camera is not dropped in rubble

HAVE CAMERA, WILL TRAVEL
The London Fire and Civil Defence Authority uses thermal image cameras to find survivors after all kinds of disasters. It sends trained teams to disaster zones, like northwestern Iran after the huge quake of June 1990.

Italian newspaper illustration from 1906 showing a boy being rescued from the remains of his home after an earthquake

Searcher wears headphones to listen for human sounds in the wreckage

TRAPPED PERSON DETECTOR
This device was used after the Armenian earthquake of 1988. Thousands of people were buried when multi-story buildings collapsed in heaps of rubble. Some were successfully located with this machine, which works by detecting vibrations.

Microphone enables rescuer to talk to trapped person

Red two-way electrode allows rescuer to converse with survivor

Yellow one-way electrode picks up vibrations

SENSITIVE NOSE
Alongside technological equipment, sniffer dogs play their part in the race to find survivors after an earthquake. The aftershocks that usually follow the main quake are a big hazard. Rescuers are often at risk as they work in the precarious remains of buildings. If an aftershock causes further collapse, the rescuers may have to be rescued too.

MEXICO CITY
Dousing flames after the Mexico City quake of 1985. Thousands died, but many more were rescued from the ruins, some days after the event.

Preparing for disaster

EARTHQUAKES AND VOLCANIC ERUPTIONS are natural events that have been happening throughout the Earth's history. As the planet's population increases, more and more people are living in danger zones, along faults or close to active volcanoes. When one of these natural events upsets human life, many people may die and their buildings and farmland may be destroyed. In the aftermath, disease and famine may be even more deadly. We cannot prevent natural disasters, but as our knowledge of the Earth's geology increases, wise planning can reduce the devastating effects of volcanoes and earthquakes. Learning to live in disaster zones means actively monitoring volcanoes and fault lines and building cities that can withstand earthquakes. It also means educating people, so that they know what to do in an emergency.

Italian magazines produced for the 1990s, the International Decade for Natural Disaster Reduction

BUILDING CITIES THAT WON'T FALL DOWN

Many modern cities are in earthquake-prone regions. One way to reduce disaster is to design buildings that can withstand the deadly shaking. The Transamerica Pyramid looks fragile, but it is designed to be twice as strong as building codes for the San Francisco Bay require. In a major quake, the structures at the base will reduce sway by a third.

LIVING IN THE SHADOW

Two thousand years after Mount Vesuvius's greatest eruption, over two million people live in the Bay of Naples in the shadow of the volcano. This is modern Herculaneum, a thriving town that surrounds the ruins of Roman Herculaneum.

FRANK LLOYD WRIGHT

A pioneer in the design of earthquake-resistant buildings, this American architect's Imperial Hotel in Tokyo survived the 1923 quake almost unscathed.

SHAKE TILL THEY DROP

Built in 1923, this innovative Japanese shaking table was used to test models of buildings to see how they stood up to severe shaking. Modern shake tables are controlled by computers.

MOST MEASURED PLACE

The town of Parkfield in central California straddles the San Andreas fault system. Seismologists have predicted a major earthquake there by the end of 1993. A laser measuring system is being used to detect movements along the fault. The laser, mounted on a hilltop in Parkfield, bounces light off a network of detectors several miles away on the other side of the fault. It can detect ground movement of less than an inch over four miles.

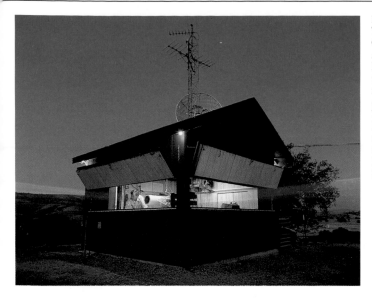

MEASURING CREEP

A technician for the U.S. Geological Survey emerges from a creepmeter. He has been measuring "creep" – slow movement along the fault. Creep releases stress along the fault without detectable shaking.

LEARNING FROM PAST DISASTERS

Earthquakes of the same size tend to happen in the same place at regular intervals. Studying large quakes – in this case, the one that rocked Pompeii in A.D. 62 (p. 47) – may help scientists to predict the next big tremor.

FALLING MASONRY

In this earthquake drill, rescue workers are treating actors "hit" by falling masonry. Many were injured by falling brick and stone in the 1989 San Francisco earthquake. Designing buildings without heavy architectural ornaments or chimneys might cut down on casualties like these.

Earthquake rescue practice in Japan

EARTHQUAKE DRILL

In Japan and California, earthquake drills are a part of everyday life. Children learn to keep a flashlight and sturdy shoes by their beds, so they can get to safety even if a quake strikes at night. Many people rush outdoors, only to be hit by falling chimneys, roof tiles, or glass. The safest place indoors is under a solid piece of furniture like a table, or beneath the frame of an archway or doorway.

Anger of the gods

AS LONG AS PEOPLE HAVE LIVED on Earth, they have been curious about natural events like earthquakes and volcanic eruptions. Myths are a way of recording or explaining these strange, often fantastic events. In many parts of the world, myths and legends handed down from generation to generation are the only history. Often these myths are not written down or have been put on the page only recently. Sometimes it is possible to recognize real places or events described in myths. Most societies at one time explained natural events as the workings of a god or gods. In this way people gave the planet the kinds of emotions we expect from humans. When the gods were angry, they punished the people with the fire of an eruption or the horrible shaking of an earthquake. Many peoples reacted to such disasters by offering sacrifices or gifts to calm the gods. Societies near active volcanoes may view the fiery mountains as the workshops of the gods (p. 36). Many gods are believed to live on the eerie summits of volcanoes, which are often shrouded in fire and cloud.

Christians in Naples try to stop the 1906 eruption of Mount Vesuvius (p. 31) with crosses and prayers

HUMAN SACRIFICE
In Nicaragua, the people once threw their most beautiful young women into the lava lake at Masaya to stop the volcano from erupting.

Lava lake

POPOCATEPETL
This Aztec illustration shows Popocatépetl, Mexico, one of the highest peaks in the Americas at 17,887 ft (5,452 m). Its name is Aztec for "smoking mountain". When the volcano erupted violently in the 1520s, the Aztecs believed the gods were angry at the Spanish conquistadores (conquerors) who had looted their temples.

RESPONSIBLE FROG
Many cultures believed that the ground they stood on was held up by some huge creature. The ancient Greeks thought the god Atlas carried the heavens (p. 10). Mongolians believed a gigantic frog held the weight. Each time the animal stumbled under his great burden, the ground shook with an earthquake. A similar Hindu myth says the Earth sits on the backs of eight giant elephants.

ONE-EYED GIANT
This is an aerial view of Mount Vesuvius. From above, such craters resemble giant eyes. They may have inspired the Greek myth of the Cyclops, a tribe of one-eyed giants who helped the fire god Hephaestus (Vulcan to the Romans) in his workshop (below; p. 36). Like craters, the Cyclops hurled fire and rocks when they were angry.

SHAKING THE SEA FLOOR
When the Greek sea god Poseidon (known as Neptune to the Romans) was angry, he banged the sea floor with his trident. This created earthquakes and tsunamis (pp. 56–57).

Destruction of Sodom and Gomorrah, by an unknown Flemish painter

SODOM AND GOMORRAH
According to the Bible, God destroyed these cities with flood and fire because he was angry at their evil inhabitants. They may actually have been devastated by some natural geological disaster.

Bronze figure of Hephaestus, first or second century B.C.

MASTER OF FIRE
The Greeks believed the god Hephaestus had his fiery workshops under volcanoes (p. 36). Another god, Prometheus, stole some of the fire from the volcanoes and gave it to humans. This myth explains how people discovered fire.

WHEN THE GODS ARE AWAY...
A Japanese myth says earthquakes are caused by the writhings of a giant catfish. Normally the gods keep the fish under control by pinning it down with a large rock. But during October, when the gods are away, the fish may get loose. This woodblock print shows the gods flying back over the ruins of Edo (now Tokyo) after a big quake in October 1855. The leader of the gods is carrying the rock.

HOME OF THE GODS
Mount Fujiyama is thought to be the home of the god Kunitokotache (p. 6). Fujiyama, the sacred spirit of the mountain, is said to protect the Japanese people. Legend says that the mountain can be climbed only by the pure of spirit. Thousands of people make the hike each year.

Did you know?

FASCINATING FACTS

In just 20 seconds, the 1991 earthquake in Kobe, Japan, damaged around 180,000 buildings, killed 6,310 people, and injured 43,000 more. It has been estimated that it will eventually cost $147 billion to rebuild the city.

Around 200 black bears were killed in the eruption of Mount St. Helens.

The effects of a volcano can be disastrous for wildlife. Figures from Mount St. Helens estimate that 11,000 hares, 6,000 deer, 5,200 elk, 1,400 coyotes, 300 bobcats, 200 black bears, and 15 mountain lions were killed by the blast.

The burning clouds of pyroclastic flows can travel at terrifying speeds of up to 300 mph (500 kph) and reach temperatures of 1,472°F (800°C), burning everything in their path.

Where cracks form in the ocean floor as tectonic plates move apart, the water heated by the magma can reach temperatures of 1,224°F (662°C).

One of Iceland's greatest attractions used to be the Great Geyser, near Rekyavik, which had a jet 200–270 ft (60–80 m) high. When the geyser stopped spouting in 1916, people managed to reactivate it a few times using soap powder, but it is now just a 60-ft (18-m) hole.

In 1883, when Krakatoa, in Indonesia, erupted, the noise was so powerful it burst the eardrums of sailors more than 25 miles (40 km) away. Around 36,000 people died, most killed by the tsunamis—some 100 ft (30 m) tall—that devastated Java and Sumatra. Villages, ships, and boats were swept inland, including a large steamer, which was found 1.5 miles (2.6 km) inland.

Fires are a major problem after an earthquake. Fractured gas pipes mean fires spread rapidly and burst water mains dry up the hoses. This, together with streets blocked with debris, make the firefighters' work very difficult.

The greatest volcanic eruption in modern times was Tambora, Indonesia, in 1815. It produced 19.2 cubic miles (80 cubic km) of volcanic ash, compared with just 0.24 cubic miles (1 cubic km) measured at Mount St. Helens. In the last 10,000 years, only four eruptions have been as violent as Tambora.

In the open ocean a tsunami can travel at incredible speeds of up to 373 mph (600 kph).

A steamer swept inland after Krakatoa erupted

Animals often show strange behavior before an earthquake. In 1975 in China, scientists successfully predicted an earthquake when they noticed snakes waking up from hibernation and rats swarming.

A truck flees from the burning clouds of Pinatubo, Philippines, 1991

At Pinatubo, pyroclastic flows traveling at more than 40 mph (70 kph) were recorded.

QUESTIONS AND ANSWERS

Q When is a volcano said to be extinct rather than dormant?

A Scientists put volcanoes into three categories. A volcano is classified as active if it has erupted within the last few hundred years. It is dormant if it has not erupted in the last few hundred years but has erupted during the last several thousand years. If a volcano has not erupted during the last several thousand years it is said to be extinct.

Q Are earthquakes high on the Richter scale the most destructive?

A Not necessarily. All sorts of factors influence the effects of a quake—the geology of the rock, in particular. Increasingly, earthquakes are measured on a scale called Moment magnitude. This combines Richter readings with observations of rock movement to give a more accurate scale of destruction.

Q How many active volcanoes are there in the world?

A There are around 1,500 active volcanoes in the world. On average, each month around 20–30 are actually erupting. Some of these are volcanoes that erupt continually, like the Hawaiian volcanoes of Mauna Loa and Kilauea.

Earthquake drill at a school

Q What should you do if there is an earthquake?

A At home, take shelter in a doorway or under a strong table. In a public place, such as a classroom, find cover under a table or desk and protect your head with your arms. When the tremors stop, leave the building, and take shelter as far as possible from walls, which may be unstable.

Q Have people ever tried to stop advancing lava flow?

A When the volcano on the Icelandic island of Heimaey erupted in 1973, the people tried to save the harbor on which the island depended. They did not stop the lava, but by spraying 6 million tons of sea water at it, they slowed it down and slightly altered its course. The lava flow stopped just 450 ft (137 m) from the harbor.

Mauna Loa, Hawaii

Q Could lava just come out of a crack in the earth?

A Yes. In 1943, in Parícutin in Mexico, a farmer found lava pouring from a crack that suddenly appeared in his field. Within a day a 33-ft (10-m) cone had formed. With eruptions over the following months, the new "mountain" grew layer by layer. After one year it was 1,476 ft (450 m) tall and had engulfed the nearby town.

A church tower rises from the lava of Parícutin.

A town buried by lava, Parícutin, Mexico

Record Breakers

BIGGEST VOLCANO
Mauna Kea in Hawaii is a massive volcano, 4,446 ft (1,355 m) taller than Mount Everest, but because it rises out of the sea bed, much of it is covered by water.

TALLEST GEYSER
The world's tallest geyser is the Steamboat Geyser in Yellowstone Park, Wyoming, with spray up to 195–380 ft (60–115 m). But in 1904, Waimangu Geyser, New Zealand, reached a height of 1,500 ft (460 m).

BIGGEST EARTHQUAKE
In 1960 an earthquake with a magnitude of 9.5 on the Richter scale was recorded in Chile. It caused tsunamis that reached Japan.

MOST DEVASTATING EARTHQUAKE
In 1556 an earthquake estimated at 8.3 on the Richter scale killed 800,000 in Shansi, China.

HIGHEST TSUNAMI WAVE
The highest tsunami wave recorded struck Ishigaki in Japan in 1971. The monstrous wave was 279 ft (85 m) high.

Timeline

Our planet has a violent history, and its constant activity continues to remind us that we live at the mercy of the natural world. The timeline below includes just some of the major volcanic eruptions and earthquakes of the past 4,000 years. We have most information about events in living memory or from records in recent history, but volcanologists can look much further back in time by studying the features of the Earth's surface. It is thought that one of the biggest eruptions ever happened 2 million years ago in Yellowstone, Wyoming, and was 250 times more powerful than that of Pinatubo in 1991.

Gas, dust, and rock explode from Mount St. Helens, 1980

1620 BCE SANTORINI, GREECE
Violent eruptions blew the island of Santorini apart and buried it under 98 ft (30 m) of pumice.

CE 79 VESUVIUS, ITALY
A burning cloud of volcanic ash engulfed the Roman towns of Pompeii and Herculaneum, killing thousands.

1755 LISBON, PORTUGAL
A powerful earthquake measuring about 8.5 on the Richter scale shook Portugal's capital, reducing it to rubble.

1783 SKAFTAR FIRES, ICELAND
A fissure (crack) 16 miles (27 km) long opened up in the Earth's surface, spewing out poisonous gasses and red-hot lava.

Craters mark Skaftar fissure today

1815 TAMBORA, INDONESIA
The biggest eruption ever recorded. Around 90,000 people were killed. It is believed that the dust ejected reduced levels of sunlight around the world and affected the climate of the planet dramatically.

1883 KRAKATOA, INDONESIA
The enormous force of Krakatoa's eruption left a crater 960 ft (290 m) deep in the ocean floor and created huge tsunamis that devastated the coastlines of Java and Sumatra.

1902 MOUNT PELEE, MARTINIQUE
All but two people out of the entire population of St. Pierre were wiped out by the burning cloud of gas and dust that raced down the sides of Mount Pelée at speeds of 100 mph (161 kph). Around 30,000 people died.

1906 SAN FRANCISCO, CA
Two huge earth tremors hit the city, setting off fires that burned for many days. The earthquake is estimated to have measured 8.3 on the Richter scale.

1920 XINING, CHINA
The entire province of Gansu was devastated when shaken by an earthquake measuring 8.6 on the Richter scale. More than 180,000 people were killed.

1923 TOKYO, JAPAN
An earthquake of 8.3 on the Richter scale flattened 600,000 homes and opened gas lines, which started a terrible firestorm.

A watch stopped by the eruption of Mount Pelée, 1902

1943 PARICUTIN, MEXICO
Lava began to flow from a crack that appeared in a farmer's field. By 1952, a lava cone stood 1,476 ft (450 m) tall there.

1963 SURTSEY, ICELAND
Undersea volcanic explosions created a new island off the southwest coast of Iceland.

1963 SKOPJE, MACEDONIA
A violent earthquake destroyed more than 15,000 homes, leaving three-quarters of the town of Skopje homeless. At least 1,000 people were killed.

The ruins of San Francisco, 1906

Cinders engulf Vestmannaeyjar, Iceland

1973 HEIMAEY, ICELAND
Eldfell volcano erupted after 5,000 years of dormancy. Molten lava engulfed one-third of the town of Vestmannaeyjar on the Icelandic island of Heimaey.

1976 TANGSHAN, CHINA
The most disastrous earthquake in modern times. A massive tremor of 8.3 on the Richter scale, centered just beneath Tangshan, almost completely destroyed the city and killed more than 240,000 people.

1980 MOUNT ST. HELENS, WA
The eruption of Mount St. Helens blew away the north side of the volcano and sent a burning cloud of gas, ash, and rock hurtling down the mountainside. Vast areas around the volcano were devastated by avalanches of rock and ice, mudflows, and floods.

1985 MEXICO CITY, MEXICO
Powerful earth tremors, measuring 8.1 on the Richter scale, shook Mexico City for three minutes. Buildings outside the center of the city were unaffected, but high-rise buildings in the city center crashed to the ground. Some 1,000,000 people were left homeless.

Kilauea volcano,
Hawaii

1985 NEVADO DEL RUIZ, COLOMBIA
The eruption of the Ruiz volcano caused a massive mudflow that engulfed the town of Armero 36 miles (60 km) away and buried 22,000 people in the mud.

1988 SPITAK, ARMENIA
Armenia and northeastern Turkey were shaken by a powerful earth tremor that almost completely destroyed the town of Spitak and killed most of the population.

1991 KILAUEA, HI
Kilauea volcano, which had been relatively gently active since 1983, suddenly produced large quantities of lava, burying 8 miles (13 km) of road, 181 homes, and a visitors' center.

1991 PINATUBO, PHILIPPINES
The most violent volcanic eruption of the twentieth century. Falling ash destroyed 42,000 homes and smothered land. Volcanic ash in the atmosphere lowered temperatures around the world.

1994 LOS ANGELES, CA
An earthquake directly under the city destroyed nine highways and 11,000 buildings in just 30 seconds.

1995 KOBE, JAPAN
Kobe was flattened by the most powerful earthquake to hit a modern city, measuring 7.2 on the Richter scale. Buildings were also damaged in Kyoto, which is about 40 miles (50 km) from Kobe.

1996 GRIMSVOTN, ICELAND
A 2.5-mile (4-km) fissure appeared in the side of the Grímsvötn volcano, which lies below the Vatnajökull glacier in Iceland. Lava melting the glacier ice caused terrible flooding, which damaged roads, pipelines, and power cables.

The destruction of an expressway, Kobe, Japan

1997 MONTSERRAT, ANTILLES
After two to three years of minor activity, a series of major eruptions left two-thirds of the island of Montserrat uninhabitable and forced 8,000 people to leave the island.

1998 NEW GUINEA
A violent offshore earthquake caused a 33-ft (10-m) tsunami, which swept 1.2 miles (2 km) inland. The tsunami destroyed four villages, and about 4,500 people died.

2002 DEMOCRATIC REPUBLIC OF CONGO
About half a million people were forced to leave their homes when rivers of lava flowed from Mount Nyiragongo. The lava took a blazing path through Goma, destroying two-fifths of the town.

Find out more

VOLCANOES ARE EXTREMELY UNPREDICTABLE and even experienced volcanologists have been killed in eruptions. However, there are volcanic national parks all over the world where you can see volcanic features first-hand, safely. There are also more accessible ways to find out more about volcanoes, including sites on the Internet where you can find news of the latest eruptions and even watch volcanic activity live.

YELLOWSTONE PARK, WYOMING
A line of people can be seen here walking through the lunarlike landscape of Norris Geyser Basin in Yellowstone National Park, Wyoming. Yellowstone lies on a volcanic hot spot and has a dramatic landscape with volcanic features such as geysers and fumaroles. It also experiences earthquakes. The park's most famous feature is the geyser named Old Faithful.

THE STORY OF AN ERUPTION
The remains of the ancient cities of Pompeii and Herculaneum, near Naples, in Italy (see pages 26–32), have not only taught scientists a lot about volcanoes, they also give visitors invaluable insight into both volcanoes and life in ancient Roman times. Both cities were destroyed when Vesuvius erupted in CE 79, but the mountain is still an active volcano—it last erupted in 1944. Weather permitting, visitors can climb up and look into the crater of the volcano.

The bodies of ancient Romans suffocated by the poisonous gases were preserved in the volcanic ash.

The ruins of Pompeii lying in the shadow of Vesuvius

Places to Visit

THE EARTH GALLERIES, THE NATURAL HISTORY MUSEUM, LONDON
Displays on volcanoes and earthquakes and the chance to experience an earthquake for yourself.

ETNA, VESUVIUS, AND STROMBOLI, ITALY
The best-known of the Italian volcanoes are Etna in Sicily, the island of Stromboli, and Vesuvius near Naples. All can be climbed with guides, weather and volcanic activity permitting.

THE CANARY ISLANDS
Volcanic features dominate the Canary Islands. Tourists can visit the active volcano on La Palma and the volcanic landscape of Lanzerote.

ICELAND
Iceland is still being formed by volcanic activity and has more than two dozen volcanoes, but is most famous for its geysers and hot springs.

Runny pahoehoe lava flowing over a cliff made up of layer upon layer of lava.

VISITING VOLCANOES
There are national parks worldwide where visitors can see signs of volcanic activity, past and present. Some of the best known are in Hawaii, Wyoming, Washington state, Iceland, New Zealand, Japan, Mexico, and the Canary Islands. In Hawaii, there is almost constant volcanic activity. Visitors can drive to the rim of the active volcano, Kilauea, walk through a lava tube, and see an eruption.

Lava flow from Kilauea volcano in Hawaii

WATCHING THE EARTH

Bᴇᴄᴀᴜsᴇ ᴏꜰ ᴛʜᴇ ᴅᴀɴɢᴇʀs, only trained volcanologists can monitor volcanoes closely, but on the Internet you can follow much of the work that such experts are doing all over the world. In the box below you will find the addresses of some Web sites with general background information on volcanology and links to lots of specific volcanoes. Some sites even have "volcano cams" so that you can watch volcanoes live, or almost live, online. For the most up-to-date information, the Smithsonian Institution produces an online weekly report on volcanic activity worldwide.

LIVING WITH A VOLCANO
These children are learning about Sakurajima volcano in Japan. It is one of the most active volcanoes in the world, erupting around 150 times a year. Like many other active volcanoes, Sakurajima is monitored by a volcano observatory that collects data for research and to help predict activity that might endanger people's lives. Most observatories have Web sites with the latest information and pictures.

WATCHING FROM SPACE
This picture was take by a space shuttle and shows thick clouds of ash and dust from the eruption of Kliuchevskoi volcano in Russia, in 1994. Volcanic ash clouds can cause pollution and affect climate and aviation. They are watched and measured by satellites. Amazing views of volcanoes on Earth and in space can be found on several Web sites.

USEFUL WEB SITES

- Volcano World:
  volcano.und.edu/vw.html
- Worldwide volcanic reference map:
  geo.mtu.edu/volcanoes/world.html
- Smithsonian Institution report on volcanic activity:
  www.volcano.si.edu/gvp/usgs/index.htm
- Volcanoes in the Learning Web:
  volcanoes.usgs.gov
- Volcano section of a site with views of the solar system:
  www.solarviews.com/eng/tervolc.htm
- NASA directory of links to natural hazards sites including volcanoes, earthquakes, and tsunamis:
  gcmd.gsfc.nasa.gov/Resources/pointers/hazards.html

DANGEROUS WORK
This volcanologist is checking gas samples inside the crater of Mount Erebus, Antarctica. It is dangerous work, and sudden eruptions have forced people out with singed ropes and clothes. But this is just a small part of a volcanologist's work. Much more time is spent analyzing the data and advising people on the risks associated with volcanoes. There are lots of sites on the Internet where you can learn more about volcanologists' work and find out how to become one.

Glossary

AA A Hawaiian word used to describe thick, lumpy lava that forms angular lumps when cool

AFTERSHOCKS Smaller earth tremors that happen after an earthquake. These may occur for several days or even weeks after the main tremor.

ASH AND DUST In volcanology, these terms refer to the smallest fragments of lava formed when a volcano explodes. Small pieces are called ash, and the powder-fine particles are known as dust.

BASALT The most common volcanic rock. Basalt is formed by runny lavas and is dark and fine-grained.

BLACK SMOKER A volcanic hot spring on the ocean floor that spits out black water containing metal sulfides and oxides

BOMBS AND BLOCKS Large pieces of lava that are thrown out during a volcanic eruption. Bombs are slightly rounded in shape, while blocks are more angular.

CALDERA A giant crater or bowl-shaped depression at the top of a volcano, formed when the summit collapses into the volcano's magma chamber. Calderas can be many miles across.

CARBONIZE To turn to carbon. Objects that contain carbon will turn to carbon (or charcoal), rather than burn, when there is not enough oxygen available for them to burn in the usual way.

Carbonized walnuts from Pompeii

A red-hot flow of aa, Hawaii

CONTINENTAL DRIFT Continent movement caused by plate tectonics

CORE The center of the Earth, made up of dense metals, in particular iron. The inner core is solid, while the outer core is liquid metal.

CRATER Hollow depression formed when the cone of a volcano collapses inward. Also known as a caldera

CRATER LAKE Lake formed when water fills the crater, or caldera, of a volcano

DORMANT The term used to describe a volcano that has not been active for more than several hundred years but was active within the last several thousand years

The crater of Mount Vesuvius

EPICENTER The point on the Earth's surface, directly above the focus, or point of origin, of an earthquake

EXTINCT The term used to describe a volcano that has not been active for over several thousand years

FAULT A fracture in rock along which blocks of rock slide past each other

FEEDER PIPE The long tube magma passes through from the magma chamber to the surface

FISSURE A crack in the ground. A fissure eruption is one where runny lava flows from a crack in the ground.

FOCUS The point within the Earth's mantle from which an earthquake originates

A geyser in Iceland

FUMAROLE A vent or opening in the Earth's surface that emits steam or gas

GEOLOGY The study of the history and development of the Earth's crust

GEYSER A place where water that has been superheated by hot magma underground bursts up into the air.

HOT SPOT A place in the middle of a tectonic plate, rather than at the boundary, where columns of magma from the mantle rise up through the crust, creating a volcano

HYDROTHERMAL VENT A place where mineral-rich water heated by hot magma underground erupts onto the surface. Geysers, black smokers, and hot springs are all hydrothermal vents.

IGNEOUS ROCKS Rocks formed as hot magma and lava cools

INTENSITY The term used to describe the severity of the shaking experienced during an earthquake. It is usually measured using the Modified Mercalli Intensity Scale.

LAHAR A mudflow made up of large quantities of volcanic fragments and water. Also known as a mudflow

LAPILLI Small fragments of lava, formed as the magma bursts out of a volcano

LAVA Hot, molten rock that is emitted from a volcano

LAVA TUBE A tunnel of lava created when the surface of a lava flow cools and hardens to form a roof, while hot, molten lava continues to flow inside it.

MAGMA Hot, molten rock inside the Earth's mantle.

MAGMA CHAMBER Area beneath a volcano where magma builds up before an eruption.

MAGNITUDE The term used to describe the severity or scale of an earthquake. This is calculated or measured in several different ways, the most common of which is the Richter scale.

MANTLE The layer inside the Earth between the crust and the core. The mantle is 1,800 miles (2,900 km) thick.

MERCALLI SCALE The scale for measuring the intensity of an earthquake by observing its effects

MID-OCEAN RIDGE A ridge of mountains on the ocean floor formed where two tectonic plates meet

MUDFLOW A fast-moving stream of mud, water, and often volcanic ash and pumice. Also known as a lahar

NUEE ARDENTE French for "glowing cloud." The term used to describe the strange clouds of a pyroclastic flow when they are a mix of cloud and hot ash

PAHOEHOE The Hawaiian term for hot, runny lava that flows quickly and, usually, in shallow flows

PILLOW LAVA Rounded lava formations shaped when lava erupts gently under water

PLATE TECTONICS The theory that the Earth's surface is broken up into large slabs, or plates. The seven large plates and various smaller plates are constantly moving at the rate of a few inches (centimeters) a year. Most volcanoes and earthquakes are found at the boundaries of these plates.

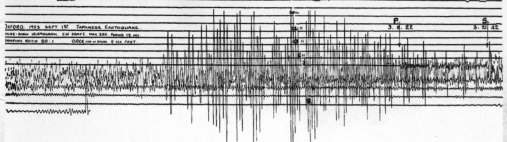

Seismogram of the 1923 Tokyo earthquake

Aa

Pahoehoe lava

PLUG An obstruction of solidified magma in the neck of a volcano

PUMICE Lightweight volcanic rock filled with holes formed by the bubbles of gas in the lava

PYROCLASTIC FLOW A burning cloud of gas, dust, ash, rocks, and bombs that flows down the mountain after an explosive eruption. If the cloud is made up of more gas than ash, it is known as a pyroclastic surge.

P WAVES The fastest and first, or "primary," waves of an earthquake

RICHTER SCALE Scale for measuring the severity of an earthquake by calculating the total energy released. This is done by studying shock waves detected by seismographs. The scale ranges from 1 to 10, with 10 the most severe end of the scale.

Pumice

RING OF FIRE The area encircling the Pacific Ocean where most volcanic and earthquake activity occurs

SEISMIC WAVES The vibrations, or shock waves, that radiate out from the focus of an earthquake

SEISMOMETER A machine for detecting earthquake shock waves is called a seismometer. A machine that records the information is called a seismograph.

SEISMOGRAM The record produced by a seismograph showing the pattern of shock waves from an earthquake

SUBDUCTION ZONE The area where two tectonic plates meet and one plate is pushed down into the mantle, becoming an explosive mix of molten rock and gas

S WAVES The slower, "secondary" waves of an earthquake

TSUNAMI A wave or series of waves caused when an earthquake or volcanic eruption disturbs the ocean floor

VENT The opening through which a volcanic eruption occurs

VOLCANOLOGIST A scientist who studies volcanoes

Volcanologists collecting gas samples on Colima volcano in Mexico

Index

Acknowledgments

The publisher would like to thank:
John Lepine and Jane Insley of the Science Museum, London; Robert Symes, Colin Keates & Tim Parmenter of the Natural History Museum, London; the staff at the Museo Archeologico di Napoli; Giuseppe Luongo, Luigi Iadicicco & Vincenzo D'Errico at the Vesuvius Observatory for help in photographing the instruments on pp. 49, 53 & 55; Paul Arthur; Paul Cole; Lina Ferrante at Pompeii; Dott. Angarano at Solfatara; Carlo Illario at Herculaneum; Roger Musson of the British Geological Survey; Joe Cann; Tina Chambers for extra photography; Gin von Noorden and Helena Spiteri for editorial assistance; Céline Carez for research and development; Wilfred Wood and Earl Neish for design assistance.

Illustrations John Woodcock **Maps** Sallie Alane Reason **Models** David Donkin (pp. 8–9, 50–51) & Edward Laurence Associates (pp. 12–13)
Index Jane Parker

Picture credits
a-above; b-below; c-center; l-left; r-right; t-top

Ancient Art & Architecture Collection: 47t. Art Directors Photo Library: 47tc, 49tc. B.F.I.: 46cr, 57cr. Bridgeman Art Library: 6tl & c. Musee des Beaux-Arts, Lille: 44tl; 44cr. British Museum: 27tr & c. Herge/Casterman: 20tl. Dr Joe Cann, University of Leeds: 25bc. Jean-Loup Charmet: 27bl, 31tl, 46bl, 51tl. Circus World Museum, Baraboo, Wisconsin: 32br. Corbis: Bettmann 67tl; Danny Lehman 65cr; Vittoriano Rastelli 70tc; Roger Ressmeyer 71br; Jim Sugar Photography 67b. Eric Crichton: 41tr, 41bl. Culver Pictures Inc: 60br. Earthquake Research Institute, University of Tokyo: 63cr. Edimedia/Russian Museum, Leningrad: 28cl. E.T. Archive: 49c, 58tr, 62tl. Mary Evans Picture Library: 8tc, 16tl, 26tl, 27br, 28c, 29cr, 46tl, 64cr, 66br. Le Figaro Magazine/Philippe Bourseiller: 19t, 19cl, 19bl, 19br, 35tr. Fiorepress: 49br. Gallimard: 44tr. G.S.F.: 13tl, 14bl; /Frank

Fitch: 20c. John Guest c.NASA: 44bl. Robert Harding Picture Library: 12tl, 14tr, 15cr, 17tr, 17cr, 20tr, 21br, 63br, 24tl, 38br, 39br, 40tr, 42c, 43br, 48br, 49bl, 51tr, 60lc, 62bl, 62-63c, Explorer 66bl. Bruce C. Heezen & Marie Tharp, 1977/c.Marie Tharp: 11c. Historical Pictures Service, Inc.: 10cr. Michael Holford: 22tr. Illustrated London News: 60bl. ImageState: 68bc. Katz Pictures: Alberto Garcia/Saba 64b. Frank Lane Picture Agency: 23rct, 23c. Archive Larousse-Giraudon: 32cl. Frank Lane Picture Agency/S.Jonasson: 41tc, 49cr; /S.McCutcheon: 57c. London Fire Brigade/LFCDA: 58bl. Mansell Collection: 31tr. N.A.S.A.: 24bc, 55cr, 68-69. Natural History Museum: 34tl. National Maritime Museum: 8tl. Orion Press: 7tr, 61bl. Oxford Scientific Films/Colin Monteath: 69br; /NASA: 69cl; /Kim Westerkov: 11bl; 15tl. Planet Earth Pictures/Franz J.Camenzind: 7cr; /D.Weisel: 17br; /James D. Watt: 23rcb; /Robert Hessler: 25tr, 25lc. Popperfoto: 6b, 11tr, 54tl. R.C.S. Rizzoli: 48lc. Rex Features: 67tr. Gary Rosenquist: 14tl, 14br, 15tr, 15br. Scala: 7c, 49bl(inset); /Louvre: 63tr. Science Photo Library/Earth Sattelite Corp.: 7tl; /Peter Menzel: 7br, 20br,

46cl, 65bl; /David Parker: 13tr, 61tl, 61tr, 65tc; /Ray Fairbanks: 18c; /Inst Oceanographic Sciences: 24c; /Matthew Shipp: 24bl; /NASA: 35c, 43cr, 44cr, 44c, 44-45b; /U.S.G.S.: 45tr; /Peter Ryan: 55tr; /David Weintraub 66t. Frank Spooner Pictures: 8cl, 16cr, 17tl, 22bl, 23tr, 23br, 35tc, 42cl, 47cl, 49cl, 56tl, 56c, 56bl, 58tl, 59tr, 59bl, 59br, 61lcb; /Nigel Hicks 69tr. Syndication International: 31cr; /Inst. Geological Science: 32tc, 35br, 41tl, 47br; /Daily Mirror: 54tr, 57tr. Susanna van Rose: 39bl. Woods Hole Oceano-graphic Institute/Rod Catanach: 24br; /Dudley Foster: 25bl; /J.Frederick Grassle: 25tc; /Robert Hessler: 25tl. ZEFA: 9tl, 21t, 34bl, 45br, 57br.

Jacket credits
Back: Bridgeman Art Library, London/New York, br.
Front: Douglas Peebles Photography/Alamy, b; NASA/Science Photo Library, tc; Bettmann/Corbis, tr.

All other images © Dorling Kindersley. For further information see: www.dkimages.com